21st Century Executive Life

by

Dr. Raymond Leslie Newkirk

Table of Contents

We can secure data and systems but the Insider Threats are the nightmares of the worse kind.

Systems Management Institute, 6347 Goethe St., Unit 105 Orlando, FL 32835.

This book is available at a special discount when ordered in bulk quantities. For information, contact Publications Sales Department, 6347Goethe St. Unit 105 Orlando, FL 32835 Tel: (407) 864 7756. www.smirsp.com[1].

www.drraynewkirk.com

1. http://www.smirsp.com

Dedication

For:
Felicisima, a Wonderful Wife & Mother,
& Maria Dorothy Calma Newkirk,
Our Great Joy

Acknowledgments

This book culminates more than 35 years reflection about the application of Systems Thinking to Leadership Development and Enterprise Design. I originally conceived of this book as the Founder of the Systems Management Institute during my studies at the Saybrook Institute in San Francisco, CA. with Bela Banathy, Arne Collen, Dennis Jaffe, and later with my colleague and friend Gene Kerfoot at the Fielding Institute in Santa Barbara.

This work was not completed in isolation. Without a doubt it is a labor of love. First and foremost, I very much appreciate the love, encouragement, and support of my wife Felicisima. I could not have gotten started on this project without her interest.

I also acknowledge the daily struggles of friends, clients, and colleagues who ignited my curiosity about the contemporary gap in management thinking and executive performance. Their comments about the emerging trends in Continuous Performance Management (CPM) first caught my attention and sparked an interest in the current problem of enterprise leadership and innovation. Although they are too many to thank individually, I am grateful for the trust and confidences they shared with me regarding their observations.

High on my list, I am grateful to my colleague Gene Kerfoot for sharing his insights and friendship the last decade of his life. I enjoyed our stimulating conversations and will carry them with me the remainder of my life and into the next. They have become some of my fondest memories of the 1990s. I will always cherish Gene's encouragement in writing this book series. I especially thank Gene for his insight on the nature of competence and his many contributions in advancing my understanding of adult learning and, of course, for revitalizing my interest in Clinical Psychology as a Psychotherapist.

I am indebted to all of those who shared their stories with me over the years. They laid the cornerstone of this work. I thank all of the many educators, consultants, and employees I have met during my formal education at the Saybrook Institute formerly in San Francisco, California and now in Los Angeles. I learned a lot about Design

Inquiry from them. I am grateful to the expatriates I worked with in the Kingdom of Saudi Arabia. Their questions encouraged me to become deeply involved in the design of Competency-Based Systems long before the Internet. Their stories of exhaustion, disappointment, and frustration led to many of the insights elaborated here. I Thank You All!

Preface

Adding people to an organization or transferring them out of an organization changes the culture of that organization. Imparting new knowledge changes culture. Changes in the structure, environment, or processes of a culture change that culture. Even the emotional transformation of a single member of a team changes the culture of that team. Change is everywhere. As the Greek philosopher Heraclitus (c. 500 BCE) told us more than 25 centuries ago, we cannot walk into the same river twice, change is every day. Change is continual. Just like that river of long ago, we cannot walk into the same organization twice. We and the world we live in, our reality, experience a continuous process of transformation. Change is inevitable. Even the people who do not like change, change. Learn to take charge of it.

The point here is that cultures are forever in flux. We cannot prevent a culture from evolving. However, we can guide the direction of such inevitable change. This is Evolutionary Leadership, or Leadership by Design. Functioning as an Evolutionary Guidance System, enterprise leadership can guide the evolutionary unfolding of an organization. In precisely this way, leaders guide the evolution of an organization from one state of culture to another. This is the best anyone can do. Think about it. As you do so, learn to leverage the power of change to defuse the treats of Cyber Terror. This will be one change that you can live with comfortably. Life is like a roller-coaster more often than we ever imagine.

Compelled by my driving interest in the success of other people, I am very much interested in the nature of Leadership and the leaders who attain the heights of Leadership success, something I call Ulthule™, my unique expression.

I think that it is interesting to note that over the years, I have found that the great majority of these leaders are unknown, unrecognized, and hidden behind the scene. For every great leader who is honored by peers and strangers alike, a dozen leaders carry him or her on their shoulders to savor the glory. This is no accident. For the hallmark of great Leadership is not fame, but it is actually evolutionary unfolding and design competence. This may not be where your prejudices lie, and it may be contrary to your opinions, common wisdom, or even your gut intuition. Nevertheless, it is the reality of leaders that they guide the evolutionary unfolding of their teams and organizations by unleashing the power of their design competence.

I have been deeply interested in people having a wonderful life for as long as I can remember. I like it a lot when things go well for others. What about you? I love the feeling of being around happy people, excited people, vibrantly joyful people, and involved people. I like to see people strive, grow, reach, yearn, and yes find satisfaction in the striving, growing, reaching, and yearning. Being part of a great experience like this is beyond mere satisfaction. And it is all the more exciting to see people achieve their dreams and become better for it. Life throws so much at us every day that it takes a lot of personal something for us to strive for achievement in spite of the obstacles that life brings our way. Think about it.

Compelled by my driving interest in the success of other people, I am very much interested in the nature of leadership and the leaders who attain the heights of leadership, something I call UlThule™, an expression I coined for lack of a better word.

Even more Interesting, over the years, I have found that the great majority of these leaders are unknown, unrecognized, and hidden behind the scene. For every great leader who is honored by peers and strangers alike, a dozen leaders carry him or her on their shoulders to savor the glory. This is no accident. For the hallmark of great leadership is not fame but evolutionary unfolding and a design competence that enables organization success even in this Age of Cyber Terror.

1: Introduction

Compelled by my driving interest in the success of other people, I am very much interested in the nature of Leadership and the leaders who attain the heights of Leadership success, something I call Ulthule™, my unique expression. For every great leader who is honored by peers and strangers alike, a dozen other leaders carry him or her on their shoulders to savor the glory. This is no accident. For the hallmark of great Leadership is not fame, but it is actually evolutionary unfolding and design competence. This may not be where your prejudices lie, and it may be contrary to your opinions, common wisdom, or even your gut intuition. Nevertheless, it is the reality of leaders that they guide the evolutionary unfolding of their teams and organizations by unleashing the power of their design competence.

One cannot adequately understand the craft of Leadership as the function of any number of psychological traits or the results of project-oriented behaviors in which the attainment of some goal defines one's leadership quotient. Rather, Leadership is a constantly evolving something that never reaches its horizon. It is forever an unfinished expression of the human heart to transcend the current substance and shape of the world. As such, Leadership, authentic Leadership, forever remains incomplete and perennially unfolding. Authentic Leadership is more about the wonder of Evolutionary Consciousness and the design of Human Activity Systems than it is about a single success or a collection of personality traits or any number of psychological descriptions that are most often discussed by the Leadership "experts" in the many books available today.

Contrary to where your prejudices lie, contrary to your opinions, common wisdom, or gut intuition, Leadership is paradoxical. Whenever it is at its closet, it is always far off. The craft of Leadership cannot be properly understood as the function of any number of psychological traits or the results of project-oriented behaviors in which the attainment of some goal defines one's leadership quotient. Rather, leadership is a constantly evolving something that never reaches its horizon. It is forever an unfinished expression of the human heart to transcend the current substance and shape of the world.

One cannot adequately understand the craft of Leadership as the function of any number of psychological traits or the results of project-oriented behaviors in which the attainment of some goal defines one's leadership quotient. Rather, Leadership is a constantly evolving something that never reaches its horizon. It is forever an unfinished expression of the human heart to transcend the current substance and shape of the world. As such, Leadership, authentic Leadership, forever remains incomplete and perennially unfolding. Authentic Leadership is more about the wonder of Evolutionary Consciousness and the design of Human Activity Systems than it is about a single success or a collection of personality traits or any number of psychological descriptions that are most often discussed by the Leadership "experts" in the many books available today.

This book breaks free from the well-traveled path of common thinking on the nature of Leadership and leaders. It carries the reader along a new journey that clarifies the wider Leadership landscape and the broader method of redesigning this landscape again and again. As we make this journey from common wisdom to Evolutionary Leadership, we find that the authentic leaders, those people who mastered the test of time, designed great Human Activity Systems. It is these great Human Activity Systems that are best suited to neutralize the terrible threats of Cyber Terror.

Whether the leader was Thomas Jefferson, Mohandas Gandhi, or other persons you personally know, they all designed highly effective Human Activity Systems, and they all exhibited a taste for evolutionary consciousness. This is monumental. They all had vastly different Intelligence Quotients, different psychological characteristics, and of course, different personality traits. Unsurprisingly, a large number of leaders even failed to achieve their goals in their lifetimes. Nevertheless, their Leadership Consciousness survived them.

For those of you who have become quite knowledgeable about Leadership, and there is a lot to know, I caution that some of you are about to enter unfamiliar territory. As you progress through this book, from short chapter to short chapter, you will gain a fresh insight into the nature and promise of Leadership. Hopefully, you will develop a Living Systems perspective on what it means to be a leader. So, sit back and enjoy the experience now presented to you. You are about to build a personal model of 21st Century Leadership designed to neutralize Cyber Terror. Enjoy the challenge. You will discover in these pages what you have probably suspected: Authentic Leadership is as rare as it is challenging. Great Leadership emerges in those who remember that "Repetitio est Mater Studiorum."

Repetition is the mother of study. Hard earned experience gained over the years has taught me that I generally need to repeat myself three or four times before a C-Level executive hears me for the very first time. Although we have two ears and only one mouth, many people at the pinnacle of decision making operate as if things were the other way around. Understanding this principle of executive enlightenment, I have designed this book to make full use of my insights into professional communications. Hoping to get across several important themes, I occasionally repeat myself with all careful deliberation. Thus, if you come across something that looks vaguely familiar, or if you find yourself wondering whether you have read something very similar elsewhere in the book, don't get alarmed. I have probably mentioned it earlier. This time, however, I will have gone deeper into the topic or perhaps have mentioned the topic from a different point of view. After all, this book is designed as a system that engages the dynamics of feedback and feedforward and convergence and divergence. As you read this book, it will become an extension of your intellectual and conceptual life.

It is time to get serious about the future of Leadership. Problems and challenges abound, even where they once seemed solved. The record confirms my suspicions: This year's solution is next year's problem. I remember one pleasant Florida evening back in 1977 discussing the future with Bud Parrish, a close friend and outstanding executive. We concluded that if the human race could make it through the 1980s without a nuclear nightmare, we would have it made. Life would finally become safe. Guess what? We certainly were naïve; no nuclear nightmare and the world became a lot more dangerous regardless of Bud and Ray.

While the world becomes exponentially more dangerous every year, our national leaders fail to grasp it all. In many cases, experts offer opinions as solutions while failing to remind the public that many of the world's current plate of problems is new to them as well. For experts and non-experts alike, the complexities of contemporary life are indeed unique. The fundamental problem for us today is that we have very little experience, if any, with solving the types of problems that urgently challenge us. Being a human being is difficult. We are paradoxical creatures - forward living and backward thinking. We talk about the future but know only the past.

Today, many talk about the paradigm shift. Books are being written about it. They argue that at the dawn of the 21st Century, executives require new models of business organization and styles of leadership to offer hope of human progress. While some executives transform their enterprises into learning organizations via new models derived from the systems paradigm, others adopt the organic or biological perspective as the preferred metaphor for describing the human condition. Even the most cursory observer understands that "something is afoot," as Holmes would say, and they would be right. That something is, of course, CYBER TERROR. That's right, you read me correctly, CYBER TERROR.

While interested persons encounter a wave of books on the new paradigm in business (about 120 a month), the lack of depth about Cyber Security, Insider Threat Prevention, does not minimize the danger of CYBER TERROR. Essentially, the wave of books available today, does not satisfy the curiosity of leaders in any essential way. They may be interesting; they may be informative; they may even be enjoyable and entertaining, but this does not make them helpful or even useful. CYBER TERROR is a chilling subject that has Cyber Security managers talking to themselves. After all, who else will listen? The full scope of today's events in Cyber Security is hidden behind a veil of commercialism and under- conceptualisms called "Social Media". Here, the reader is likely to remain ignorant about the more important aspects of the current paradigm shift, and what it truly means to his or her life.

Even when they hear about it, they refuse to believe it. As Phillips once observed, the reader may not be aware that the current discussions over the paradigm shift "are related to those over System Theory, over organicism in biology and psychology, over structuralism and functionalism, and over internal relations in philosophy. Think "CYBER TERROR".

When we add to this the conflicts over "the search for meaning in the organization" and the avoidance of depth by most authors of Leadership and Management books, we can readily conclude that confusion is the hallmark of the today's developed society. I know of at least one best seller in the management category that never exceeded seven words per sentence. In fact, the author, someone I personally knew, confided that any sentence with more than seven words became too complicated to reach the minds of the intended audience, business leaders of America.

While a clear statement on the central ideas of the current age is difficult to find, failure, insecurity, instability, anxiety, hopelessness, helplessness, waste, cynicism, and all the rest are consuming this and the generation to come. In the fray, we continue to miss great opportunities for human achievement. Moreover, we will eventually discover that the worst lessons of history will indeed repeat themselves if we continue to avoid our responsibility through ignorance or choice to guide our own evolutionary unfolding to attain a positive outcome.

The concept of paradigm shift is difficult to explain because we are often imprisoned by the paradigm we need to escape. This is one reason Cyber Security is so difficult to address. People experience great difficulty envisioning the state of the new situation. Unfortunately, the pundits of the paradigm shift characterization of modern life often fail to explain what it is they mean by paradigm shift. From what, for example, are we shifting? And to what? What philosophical challenges and psychological presuppositions are implied in this shifting scene? Moreover, are we merely revisiting well- traveled territory dressed in a new landscape, a repackaging of familiar goods so op speak? Or, are we actually moving into a new dimension of human understanding, and with everything this may mean, good and bad?

For example, perhaps the new shift is only the received view of life obscured by the good intentions of under-conceptualized technological innovation? Better yet, maybe the recent shift is ancient thinking rediscovered by amateur exploration and entrepreneurial spirit? The point here is: Have we been here before? Is this happening again?

My experience tells me that the paradigm shift is probably all of these. For example, the Tribune Meneius Agrippa successfully introduced the organic analogy, an important aspect of the paradigm shift, in his effort to quell an outbreak of civil disobedience long before Miller (1978) wrote his great work Living Systems. The longer we endure, the more we demonstrate that nothing under the sun is new. Disappointing, right? Should not human life achieve more than simple endurance recycled through the "same old same old"?

This work presents a framework for assisting us with answering many of the questions posed above. It examines the core issues of emerging thought in evolutionary leadership and clarifies a few of the more significant implications of this thought in the modern extremely technical enterprise. This book encourages leaders to get serious about a lot of things in their lives, and the lives of those in their care. After all, it is not much of a secret that the first thing many executives forget is their concern for their people. Surprise, surprise!

Although this book is not large, it covers an enormous body of thought. I wrote it in the belief that we can discuss the stinging issues of this age while solving important problems that impact business performance, strategic productivity, and human worth. In its totality, this book presents an organizing perspective, termed Vision 21®, to guide our thinking about the impact of Cyber Terror on organization performance. It introduces an operational framework and design methodology to guide us through the challenge of transforming the essence of leadership and management in an enterprise culture assaulted by Cyber Terror. While the systems perspective informs the strategic framework, Vision 21® lays the foundation for the design of state-of-the-art business processes and executive level Evolutionary Guidance Systems, the EGS.

The Modern Triumvirate

In Ancient times, the Romans had their Triumvirates. The First noteworthy Triumvirate included Julius Caesar, Pompey and Crassius, the rich. The second consisted of Antony, Lepidus, and Octavian in 43 BC. Although unofficial, these triumvirates changed History. The moral here, of course, is that it doesn't take many people to upset the apple carts of history, and it does not take forever either. Today, a few people can spend very little time working on their own agenda and destroy a large corporation. This is "Executive Life in the 21st Century" because of the toxicity of CYBER TERROR. Just two words and the hair on my arms stands up. They are indeed frightening words, especially when they are activated by even a single Cyber Terrorist working alone through the cover and protection of carelessly granted unearned "Trust". What a disguise this is. Simply heart wrenching.

The 21st Century Triumvirate

Today, executives face another Triumvirate that can also become a killer. It might not include Julius Caesar, but it does include Leadership, the Organization, and CYBER TERROR. I capitalize this third component to ensure that it is not overlooked. Many executives scan so much important stuff so rapidly these days, I simply want you to pause, if only for a few seconds, and reflect on your organization's Cyber Security and Insider Threat Risk Management situations.

In developed societies, people generally live their lives as a quest for convenience. On the other hand, biologists would say that life is a quest for energy. Modern human beings participate in this quest for convenience by engaging in commerce. Education, Health Care, Manufacturing, Information Systems and Technologies, Food Distribution, and the Optical Business, among others, represent different forms of commercial enterprise geared to an improved quality of life through improved convenience. The formula here is simple: The greater the convenience, the greater the generation of profits. Since many of these industries each surpass billions of dollars in annual revenues, they occupy an influential position of business leadership in the commercial environment. This is the dream of the many executives who fill Leadership positions, especially in the most influential enterprises.

Today, everyone needs good products, and they need them quickly, cheaply and conveniently. Efficiency represents the ultimate quest for convenience. However, with the notable exception of a few mass merchandisers, discount chains, and the all too few innovative grocers who generally sell their goods at approximately 22% less than the average grocery store, the dream for an inexpensive and efficient supply of products goes unrealized.

This work examines the leadership environment of the 21st Century and examines how it may deliver products and services inexpensively and efficiently to everybody while increasing profits. As an approach to working efficiently, business enterprise eagerly adopted or refined a family of strategies as Best Practices termed Virtual Commerce or simply VC. At the time of adopting these "Best Practices", trade experts expected VC to reduce prices to consumers by up to 11% or more in some industries and rapidly. A number of industries. For example, a few of the most efficient companies ceased being the most effective companies. Imagine that! Surprise, surprise! It seems that in the drive to become ever more efficient, they adopted Business Process Re-engineering (BPR) to downsize their organizations. Eventually so many companies downsized their organizations that many employees became ex-employees. Information Systems replaced the work that a notable number of human employees formerly earned a living doing. Imagine. As a result, economic growth of the nation decreased because less people earned an income. In this case, technological progress did not deliver worker progress. Time wounds all heels. So, this was happening during the last couple of decades of the 20th Century. Many people were developing strong attitudes against emerging Information Technologies and the systems they enabled. I wonder why?

So here we are. Time to explore 21st Century Leadership from the Systems Perspective. In an effort to keep this book on the reliability path forward, I echo the admonition of Arthur O. Lovejoy who summed up the current age of the paradigm shift:

> "You may—I say it again—find much of the thinking of an individual, a school, or even a generation, dominated and determined by one or another turn of reasoning, trick of logic, methodological assumption, which if explicit would amount to a large and important and perhaps highly debatable proposition in logic or epistemology".

As such, leadership, authentic leadership, forever remains incomplete and perennially unfolding. Today, authentic leadership is more about the wonder of Evolutionary Consciousness and the design of Human Activity Systems than it is about a single success of a single industry or a collection of personality traits or any number of psychological descriptions that identify Insider Cyber Threats.

This book breaks free from the well-traveled path of traditional thinking on the nature of Leadership and leaders. It carries the reader along a new journey that clarifies the wider Leadership Landscape and the broader method of safely redesigning this landscape again and again. As we make this journey from common wisdom to Evolutionary Leadership, we find that the authentic leader, that person who mastered the test of time, designed great Human Activity Systems. Some were quite evolutionary.

Whether the leader was Thomas Jefferson, Mohandas Gandhi, or someone you personally know, or have known, they all were great designers of Human Activity Systems, and they all exhibited a taste for Evolutionary Consciousness. This is monumental. They all had vastly different Intelligence Quotients, different psychological characteristics, and, of course, even different personality traits. Some leaders even failed to achieve their goals during their lifetimes. Nevertheless, their Leadership Legacy survived them.

For those of you who know a lot about leadership, I congratulate you on your good fortune. I also caution you to remember that there is more about leadership that you do not know than you do know. For the rest of you, I suggest that you are about to enter unfamiliar territory. As you progress in this book from chapter to chapter, you will gain a fresh insight into the nature of leadership and develop a living systems perspective on what it means to be a leader. So, sit back and enjoy the experience ahead. You are about to build a personal model of 21st Century leadership. Enjoy the challenge.

"Repetitio est Mater Studiorum."

The focal point of Virtual Commerce (VC) is the consumer. The theory here is that when Best Practices achieve critical mass as an increasing number of participants implement this family of VC strategies, experts expect the VC program to reduce the cost of business operations just as significantly. Although executives understand the value of less expensive business operations, the thrust of VC consists directly in business growth as an industry response to the end consumer and indirectly the reduction of cost in the supply chain. Doesn't this sound simply wonderful. Here is the fundamental formula:

> Efficient Business Practices (EBP) plus Virtual Commerce (VC) minus Human Resources equals Business Growth (BG). Or EBP + VC - HR = BG.

After working in a multitude of industries and experiencing the confusion that new initiatives generally incite within industries, I wrote this book to update Leaders and other Executives about the problem with this widely adopted Formula. This family of EC strategies currently employed globally as defined by several industry-wide joint working committees is inadequate as it stands. What Leaders and some Executives commonly fail to do here in this very dynamic 21st Century is quite obvious. They fail to locate this formula in the wider context of the changes now occurring in management thinking and business practice. The changes that I refer to are the ones that embed CYBER TERROR within specific locations and environments within the enterprise. The actual formula would be more accurate: EBP + VC – HR + IT = CT + IBO, meaning: Efficient Business Practices (EBP) plus Virtual Commerce (VC) minus Human Resources plus Insider Threats equals CYBER TERROR plus Insecure Business Operations.

What a difference! Cyber Insecurity is a serious threat to an enterprise. Indeed, the elimination of CYBER TERROR has become a core concern for Leaders and Executives everywhere. Indeed, CYBER TERROR negatively impacts their budgets, their Business Plans, their hiring practices, their training programs, their internal workplace relationships, their workplace access rules and regulations, employee related personal property controls, their security procedures and processes and systems and Cyber Security standards and procedures, the designs of their various work places, the rules and regulations governing property management and governance, on and on and on. I am sure you get the point. Cyber Security is serious, expensive, elaborate, and life changing. It alters the workplace in many known and hidden ways. CYBER TERROR is no joke and many people respond to it using inadequate Cyber Security programs.

This book constitutes an important work about 21st Century Leadership practice. I cannot overstate the critical nature of VC and its impact on the economic health and success of your company in the coming years. If you wish to remain a serious participant in the evolving business climate, your time is long overdue for becoming comfortable with the VC vision, its mission, goals, and strategies. The ideas expressed in this book are already becoming second nature to executives wishing to lead their companies well into the 21st Century as serious competitors. I begin this book by discussing my Electronic Commerce vision termed Effective Business Response (EBR). I then introduce the specific strategies and requirements of the EBR Program that highly competitive executives are presently employing in their organizations. I refer to my own approach to EBR implementation as Vision 21®. The language, terminology, expressions, and definitions used throughout this book come directly from industry practices, associated trade groups, and the paradigm of General Systems Inquiry. Although we should become familiar with the official jargon of our own industry whenever we can, I substitute non-technical expressions wherever feasible. If you cannot digest the terminology, you should encourage your particular trade group to produce something more appropriate.

EBR via Vision 21® provides my response to the postmodern initiative for Electronic Commerce. I fashioned Vision 21® from more than 35 years of practical experience seasoned with advanced academic work in behavioral and management science, systems inquiry, organization inquiry, clinical psychology, management science, information systems, and the philosophy of science. Through Vision 21®, postmodern organizations offer an ever-improved value to consumers and stock-holders. Vision 21® empowers your organization to provide exceptional products to valued customers by building Effective Business Relationships using evolutionary business practices.

Throughout this book, I prefer the viable concept of Business Intelligence Group (BIG) over Information Services Department (ISD) because success in today's business environment demands much more than the management of information systems and their related technologies. Today, executives are challenged to become very good at using information as a genuine business asset of substantial worth. Executives with "Foresight" realize now the need to move beyond the data, information, and knowledge paradigms to embrace the challenge of executive wisdom. The Business Intelligence Group paradigm moves beyond the unrealistic task of sustaining competitive advantage by providing the business leverage to succeed in a climate marked by the forces of hyper-competition.

The Business Intelligence Group model directly contributes to the bottom line via the real-time movement and management of accurate, timely, and accessible hyper-information that adds value to the product portfolio. BIG is more than information technology, management information reporting, automated data processing, or information management. In sum, the Business Intelligence Group:

- Leverages the capability to generate rapid online business solutions that accelerate the delivery of leading-edge products, processes, relationships, and profits.
- Enables business strategies, competitive leverage, and growth.
- Enables the core information process to integrate an entire enterprise while linking that enterprise with its markets.

- Delivers flexibility and connects products with customers.

Business success demands resiliency. While the principal trends of technology deliver improved management capabilities via their traditional support roles, they do not ensure resiliency. The BIG moves beyond this by virtue of its charter as the core business process that generates earnings as a component of the information asset. While others discuss the role of Information Technology (I/T) and Management Information Systems (MIS) in support of the core business processes, the BIG establishes the business information flow as a core business process directly contributing to the bottom line. This means that the BIG offers more than technology as an enabler of the organization; it offers knowledge and intelligence as an asset with product value. The BIG offers a view on the value of information that differs from the one commonly understood. This book series outlines an EC empowered enterprise model as a business and Information Technology strategic action tool.

The BIG fully understands that while efficiency is about machines; effectiveness is about people. Although EC empowers core business processes and ideally passes the savings to consumers, in itself it remains insufficient to navigate the difficult times of a hyper-competitive era threatened by CYBER TERROR. In a world plagued by Insider Cyber Security Threats, doing the right thing is more important than doing things right. If you believe that you are protected from the forces of CYBER TERROR because you are in a slow turn industry, guess again. EC as an approach to sustaining competitive advantage seriously conflicts with another, and less cooperative, management movement, that termed Disruption, the gift of CYBER TERROR.

I am concerned about CYBER TERROR and what it means to Leaders and Executives and their business partners. If it is true that the rule today is that there are no rules, as indicated by the behaviors of Amazon, Google, Facebook and Apple, how can any enterprise bank on EC to sustain competitive advantage when cyber security can be so problematic? Advancing the vision of EC in today's hypercompetitive world, I developed Vision 21®. While EC focuses on efficiency, Vision 21 concentrates on effectiveness. In a hyper-competitive world, we do not want to perpetuate the current strategies that do the wrong thing right.

I designed Vision 21® to minimize the risks inherent in EC by assisting executives with the difficult challenge of doing the right thing right. This book will better enable you to decide what to do when the strategic practice of Disruption sidetracks your business goals. With Vision 21® to guide your implementation of EC, your enterprise will enter the world of Virtual Commerce more securely.

VC empowers an enterprise to engage in business globally 24 hours a day, seven days a week while minimizing sunk costs. E-Commerce is the foundation for Virtual Commerce. Vision 21® is the framework for Effective Business Relationships. Together, VC and EBR opens the way to hyper-growth in global competition.

2: Leadership in the Age of Cyber Terror

I divided this work into several parts. Part One, consisting of the first eleven chapters, moves into the 21st Century by describing the new world facing those at "the Pinnacle of Decision Making". Introducing a new model of leadership action and executive practice, Part One illuminates the path to Reconstructed Leadership, the secret ingredient in the recipe of meaningful success. Part One provides the foundation for Part Two.

The first several chapters discuss the changing world of the C-Level executive. In total, they present a model of the executive team as an Appreciative Evolutionary Guidance System. This model describes the crucial dimensions of executive action and lays the foundation for a renewed experience of executive life. While chapter one, two and three describe the new executive, his or her vision, and the transition from Electronic Commerce to Virtual Commerce, chapters four, five six, and seven discuss 21st Century leadership strategy, the environment of Insider Theat Prevention and Mitigation, Virtual Commerce Cybersecurity Program Management, Design Inquiry, and the relationship between the Chief Information Officer and the Business Intelligence Group. Part One concludes with chapters eight, nine, ten, and eleven in which the book discusses the transition from manager to leader, the scope of the changing Leadership World, the new, and expanding, role of executive life, and finally the need to move well beyond 20th Century executive thinking and management practice.

The New Millennium Executive

Management is a difficult profession at best. At its worse, it becomes an unbelievable nightmare. Recently, I had the misfortune of suffering through an unbelievable nightmare, a really tough experience for me and everyone involved. It was the proverbial project from ignorance. You know the one that compels you to constantly look over your shoulder as you move from one crisis to another.

That project reaffirmed many of the principles I had learned throughout my life, re-taught ones that I should have never forgotten, and introduced several new lessons I probably would have never learned had I missed this great experience. Doubtlessly, I enjoyed the satisfaction of succeeding against all odds. Our team snatched success out of the jaws of defeat.

My greatest satisfaction, however, came from assisting others with expanding their professional horizons by rethinking how they will design complex projects as we continue along in this 21st Century stained by the ever-emerging challenges of Cybersecurity. You see, CYBER TERROR is very real and it is probably here to stay simply because the Cyber Terrorists is probably here to stay. Of course, the Cyber Terrorist has always been around in some form or another doing his or her thing in one form or another. What's new about this, you might ask? The stakes are new. They belong to this historical time and no other. This is because a single person acting alone, plotting in isolation, can destroy even a billion-dollar company, and do it rapidly. Simply incredible! The Dawn of a New Level of Vigilance has become a Billion Dollar necessity. Believe it or not.

As with many things in life, that project was not all bad; it had a few redeeming qualities. For one thing, it contributed to the growth of my team. We experienced every conceivable management contradiction and tripped through numerous shortcomings disguised as success. For some of us, life does not get any better than this. Who does not like to learn from experience? Ouch, really? The problem in this situation, of course, is the emotional pain we are forced to endure before we can enjoy such hard won growth. In the high-tech industry, emotional pain characterizes the workplace. Although individuals are resilient, endurable, and capable, believe me when I tell you, organizations are fragile. They have always been so. History reveals this much. Even Kings lost their heads. Just ask the French. The current threat of CYBER TERROR makes this more so than at any other time.

Cyber Terror is not a Fad

Usually, I enjoy visiting book stores. Lately, however, I have become bothered by the great number of new Leadership and Management titles that come out every year. How can a society produce so many experts with so little to say and with so little experience? The glut of ideas sold today discourages me from writing this book. But I do not offer yet another fad; nor do I intend to experiment with you, your organization, or your professional future. In this book, I simply present a potent model for effectively, efficiently, and profitably leading teams through the next few years of the 21st Century, CYBER TERROR or not.

Unlike the trends and fads of the last few years, I do not advocate re-engineering, downsizing, upsizing, business partnering, jumping the curve, estimating the cycles, riding the wave, challenging the boardrooms, jumping off the roof, or inflicting chaos. Rather, I merely encourage Executives, and those within their sphere, to take care of the basics effectively to successfully guide and grow their businesses through the muddy waters of Cybersecurity. With the advent of modern Information Technologies and their networks, and the rapid social and commercial acceptance of the Internet and social media, executives gain an improved opportunity for becoming and remaining successful than ever before. However, this is so only if they understand the strategic value of the new business tools that are essential for eliminating and blocking CYBER TERROR from infiltrating their organizations

Hypergrowth through Virtual Commerce and Cybersecurity

Recently, a few highly influential business leaders have begun to seriously discuss the fallacy of re-engineering, downsizing, and right sizing. Echoing Andy Grove, the former Chief Executive Officer of Intel, they realize that a great company cannot shrink to regain leadership success. Rather they "must" stay on top to remain great. You are a rare executive if your company loses its leadership position only to regain it later. Too many competitors hunger to replace you.

Great executives understand that regardless of the short-term euphoria associated with downsizing, companies must grow revenues to enjoy success. It's the bottom line. This means that Cybersecurity is not a free lunch. It indeed impacts the bottom line. If it does not impact the bottom line because of its cost, eventually there will not be a bottom line at all.

Rapid growth challenges the entire organization. Over the last 30 years, Dell Computers has grown phenomenally. But working there could shorten your life. The current Chief Executive Officer is beginning to appreciate this as he moves his company to adopt less painful approaches to management practice and seek new insights into leadership.

It is not lost on me that top companies, especially in high technology industries, produce even more stress than revenues. The necessity for Cybersecurity places additional stress of the revenues. Paradoxically, if the Chief Executive Officers of such high stress organizations guided their enterprises as Appreciative Evolutionary Guidance Systems, they could possibly achieve even higher profits while simultaneously reducing stress. It all comes down to vision. Guided by an innovative, noble, and in-depth vision, your enterprise will move from growth to hyper-growth, the golden apple of only a few. In entrepreneurship, we call them Unicorns. Lacking such a vision, your success will overtake you. For the uninspired executive, one not adequately responding to the omnipresent treat of Cybersecurity, the traditional path to success will ultimately breed personal and business failure, if they attain any success at all.

Thought Break One

People can be difficult to get along with, even when their managers look out for them. Implementing an Appreciative Human Systems Environment does not mean that staff appreciation will follow. On the contrary, if the design of the Human Activity System is under-conceptualized, or the executive insight over idealistic, or the political acumen inexperienced, the Appreciative Human Activity System will be anything but appreciative. I should point out that using a Systems Approach in designing an organization does not discourage a bad actor from engaging in bad actions. However, what it does do for an organization is nevertheless very important. It creates a sense of openness, cooperation, heightened awareness, and ultimately, open and more responsive communications among employees, often including people who normally keep to themselves no matter what.

Regardless of one's intention to implement the most exciting and responsive work environment possible, people will be people. Remember Agency Theory? It reminds us that people work in an organization for many different reasons and competing values. While management may project goodwill and appreciation for those in the organization, smart managers remember that some of their best people may care less about the management vision of an organization than their own hidden wishes which may conflict with those of management. In this situation, skillful managers realize that organization influence may reside elsewhere than in the Boardroom. While individuals are very strong, organizations are indeed very fragile. This makes it vital that management engage in an appropriately developed Design Inquiry during the design of the actually very robust Appreciative Human Activity System. Think about it. What is required here is a new and all-encompassing Executive Vision. One that has CYBER TERROR in its crosshairs.

3: The New Executive Vision

Even in Executive Life, the concept of Vision remains controversial even to this very day. Probably we all have heard about the supposed comments attributed to President Bush the Elder regarding this "vision nonsense". Although I am not sure that he actually uttered such words, I know from experience that a number of executives still do not get it. They speak of values but ignore vision. In so doing, executives reveal their personal constraints. Values are the foundation of vision. However, ignoring the role of vision as an instrument of action, values remain disconnected from action and merely become the fuel of corporate discussion groups.

For executives, Vision illuminates both the mission and goals of the enterprise. Vision grounds the mission by clarifying what the organization aspires to be. It defines the goals of the enterprise by identifying the achievements that form the many action plans. Thus, we can see that from the Vision the components of all organization processes emerge for which strategies and tactics are the drivers. Constrained by the vision, strategies define how management is to achieve long term goals. Moreover, tactics outline how management is to achieve the programs that support and enable the related strategies. In this sense then, vision represents the synthesis of all tactics since it is both long term and strategic.

Vision conveys values, illuminates the mission, and defines the goals. It introduces strategy and enables tactics. Without vision as an organizing framework for executive success, management drifts because it lacks guidance. Soon, a sense of arbitrariness, negative chaos, troublesome groans, discomfort, misery, ineffectiveness, and growing inefficiency begin to emerge. Inevitably, lacking an in-depth and noble vision, companies begin to retort defensively that they are at their best when things are at their worst. I have heard this groan of anguish so often that I will never forget it.

Vision means excitement, excitement about something in one's life offering greater possibilities for the future. Although visions ignite the present, they inflame an entire lifetime. Vision means connectedness, connecting the past with the future through consistency in thought and action. Visions demand more than dreams. They require an organizing view based on considerable knowledge, experience, and wisdom. Authentic Visions enrich the human heart and fuel the imagination.

An authentic Vision can be felt and experienced as well as known and articulated. Real Visions appeal to the intellect and the emotions. They are creative. Visions offer solutions and actions. They can be ignoble or noble, shallow or deep. A noble Vision links the visionary with the beneficiary, and when noble and deep enough, transforms failure into success.

Lacking a noble an in-depth vision, success ultimately denigrates into failure. Since noble visions can never be nightmares, they exceed dreams. While dreams freely stimulate conversations, enliven psychoanalysis, and often induce more sleep, visions change worlds and fully awaken the visionary. Dreams require passivity, fatigue and retreat from reality; visions demand activity, courage, and advancement.

Visions require the visionary to be fully awake. While dreams impact only dreamers, visions impact entire cultures. While dreams require only sleepers, visions require leaders and participants. Dreams require individuals, visions require teams. Executives who dismiss the value of visions often capitulate to fear or ignorance. However, visions inspire courage and hope. Lacking a noble and in-depth vision, executives remain incomplete. We know that incomplete executives never get the job done.

If noble and deep visions fuel the genesis of executive success, why do we have so many skeptics? Probably this occurs because the idea of success is so personal. One person's success is another person's failure. Perhaps, the skeptics themselves lack a noble vision that articulates the need for others in their life with whom to obtain and share success? Too many executives really do believe their own hype. MCI

WorldCom and Enron were the archetypical models of such executive hype, dishonesty really. Noble visions humble the great leaders. Since such leaders focus more on their visions than themselves, they do not even realize that they are great. Their visions are everything. Shallow visions inflate the pretenders who focus more on themselves as great leaders than on their visions. I have heard too many executives claim that they alone accomplished turnarounds. Even when they shared credit with others, they did so as a technique of manipulation rather than as an expression of gratitude.

> "In-depth and noble Visions deliver the overarching purpose that links the many dimensions of executive life. In-depth and noble Visions really are indispensable to success."

Skilled executives communicate their visions to their entire organizations at an appropriate level of priority. Since the organizing vision becomes the driver of enterprise-wide change, executives empower managers to act on the vision so that each executive achieves immediate results as (s)he formalizes the new approaches to business operations necessitated by Virtual Commerce. During the implementation process, operational managers group all gains according to type. Then they consistently evaluate them against the important cost to profit ratios. The overarching Vision assists managers with organizing the operational activities.

Cybersecurity and Your Vision

Over the years, people have told me that visions are a lot to do about nothing. A vision and three dollars will get me a cup of coffee, they lament. Or better yet, they tell me that we could have better used the time wasted to get something better done for the team rather than waste it on our discussions about vision. Such arguments leave me dumfounded. I wonder if these critics fully understand what they have actually said. More often than not, I give them the benefit of the doubt by assuming that they fail to fully grasp the nature and power of an authentic Executive Vision, and everything that goes into forming it. Visions are not dreams. I do not know but perhaps their experience of the visioning process was a poor one, or maybe they just don't get it.

I then go on to point out that the leader's vision is the organization's formative reservoir of power. Management will find their reason for acting within the vision and develop plans flowing from it. Since the vision contains the operational values of the enterprise, as the formative elements of the vision, management can turn to the vision to examine all progress and verify the integrity of management decision making. In this sense, visions are a potent contribution to management thinking and practice.

Beyond this, I remind the brave critics of vision that it is the vision that gives direction to the Mission Statement and illuminates both long and short-term goals as elements of strategy. Indeed, I remind the critics that management is fully incapable of moving the organization toward measurable action via strategies and tactics without a vision. Moreover, since the leader owns the responsibility for defining the most formative components of the vision, managers exist in a leadership vacuum without it. Visions may be global, national, corporate, and even personal. Occasionally a personal vision may be global, national, and corporate simultaneously. Fundamentally, however, visions precede strategy. They serve as the formative source of all leadership power. Fundamentally, the capability to deliver a potent vision is the key attribute of leadership.

This book offers an organizing framework for developing your own 21st Century Executive Vision. If you have gained the experience to see into the future only a little, you will see that Cybersecurity should occupy a central place in your new vision. Following upon this line of thought, an executive can still benefit from the efficiencies of Virtual Commerce today. However, this is the case only if these executives frame their desire within his or her in-depth and noble Executive

Vision to develop a hyper-growth company assured by rigorously validated Cybersecurity strategies.

As one might suppose, this vision is immense. It calls for a radical change in the way executives, as persons of great business, personal, and social responsibility, view their roles in the world of enterprise, roles now substantially impacted by CYBER TEROR, also termed CT. When I speak of Cybersecurity, I mean the highly secure and monitored business strategies, leadership visions, management approaches, structures, and systems consisting of the intelligence, knowledge, information, data, repositories, computers, networks, software, and other Information Technologies that make the highly secure, efficient, tightly integrated, modern business operations possible.

When I speak of Virtual Commerce (also termed v-commerce), I mean the infusion of e-commerce with a noble and in-depth vision to attain profitable business operations globally, 24 hours a day, seven days a week. Hypergrowth occurs whenever an enterprise grows from nothing to one billion dollars or more in revenue in five years or less. By Vision 21®, I mean an enterprise-wide, multi-domain, information management, and strategic action approach that assists executives in articulating their postmodern, secured, v-commerce enterprise visions.

Vision Building Process

Visions emerge as our personal response to the urge to do things better or to make life better for ourselves, and hopefully others. At the executive level, visions form within the environment of competitive necessity, that is, they emerge from the competitive desire to do better than the next guy. Visions are not high-level dreams or under-conceptualized yearnings. They emerge from personal depth, intelligence, wisdom, and visionary acumen. When we adequately articulate our visions, they tell others not only how our vision will work, but how well. They also tell others what things must come together and how they might or might not go right. In this sense, visions become real whenever we can clarify them from top to bottom. In visioning, as Aristotle warned us so long ago, if we do not know what to say, we do not know what we mean.

We commence the visioning process by producing an initial vision statement. Here we say how the vision will work and define the detailed visioning process. We then begin to articulate the core characteristics of the process to establish how well the vision will work. These characteristics define the flow of the process, the desired output to be achieved, the performance requirements, the technology involved in making the vision actionable, the organization of the vision itself, and the organization to be involved or impacted by the vision.

Next, we identify the performance measures and define the objectives well enough to clarify the things that have to go right. Some of these may include the cost of realizing the vision and its quality, cycle-time, and responsiveness objectives.

Along with these, we also articulate the specific critical success and failure factors of the vision to prepare for trouble ahead. The visionary should be wise enough to think about the things that might not go right and the reasons for these failures. Interestingly, success and failure factors are associated with people, technology, and products or matter, energy, and information.

Also, the executive visionary thinks a lot about the many potential barriers to vision realization. After all, a great number of implementation problems seem to shadow even the most successful visionary. Resource allocation, corporate culture, technical constraints, production issues, market conditions, skill levels, timing, and a host of other factors may inhibit the full expression of the vision.

Strategies, Processes, Vision, Objectives, & Attributes

Although authentic visionaries revel in the big picture, they clearly understand that success explodes from the details. Beginning with the big picture of the new world, the visionary quickly moves to art and the science of strategy building. After all, a vision implies a strategy. In business, vision implies a business strategy. For example, while Efficient Consumer Response (ECR) may be a grand vision, Efficient Promotions is a single business strategy of that grand vision.

After selecting the most appropriate and reasonable strategy, the visionary selects the relevant vision building process. Form here, the visionary formulates the vision's operational component to design the process that ultimately enables the vision to emerge and successfully mature. This smaller operational vision establishes the objectives and attributes that correspond to the previously designed process. In the 21St Century organization, the visionary produces a vision that optimizes the interfaces between the social and technical systems which define the workplace culture. Here the visionary presents the vision as a conceptual design model. Here, the visionary first specifies the business rules linked to the design. The visionary then analyzes the needs of the end-users and determines how these impact the workflows forming the organization.

One can see that at a very fundamental level the visioning process establishes the enterprise-wide change process. In the social dimension, the vision moves from departmental objectives, to organization redesign, and then on to information technology job design and the formulation of personnel policies. In the technical dimension, the vision moves from conceptual design to the construction of an information repository, and then to development, operational evaluation, documentation, and maintenance. The business-rule specifications, human-computer allocations, graphical end-user interface specifications, workstation designs, and implementation support processes link the social and technical systems.

Visionary Passion

Since they are more than dreams, visions do not materialize out of nowhere. Remember, dreams are for those who sleep. Visions are for those who engage life. They require an abundance of knowledge, informed intuition, and insight. Analytical skills are helpful, but intuition and synthesis are the building blocks. Beyond these prerequisites, however, the visionary is driven by something quite a bit more significant than facts and knowledge. Passion is the thing that forges visionaries. Passion drives the vision, captures the audience, and empowers those who make the vision a reality. Communications without passion is soon forgotten. With passion as the driving force, brick walls crumble, road-blocks become the path to greater advantage, and the repository of solutions deepens. Passion is the stuff out of which leadership arises to build the basic elements of the vision. From these elemental building blocks as the starting point, passion becomes the fuel which drives the evolutionary unfolding of the vision building process through which the visionary attracts the team that moves the vision from the concept stage to the reality stage.

Ignited by the vision, the visionary selects and prepares the core team that refines the vision. The leader articulates the vision, establishes the strategic consensus, communicates the vision globally, links the vision to the strategic plan, and ultimately realizes the vision. It is the leader's passion for the vision that enables the core team to define shared values, draft the mission and goals, assign other task-oriented teams, plan projects, learn new skills, and grow and survive in the self-guided and unfolding environment now being formed by the vision. It is the leader's passion that enables the team to make the vision a reality and commit to in-depth planning, engage in near-term tasks, and succeed during the long-term roll-out. Table 2.1 below guides the visionary in the formulation of an in-depth and noble vision.

Table 2.1 Strategic Program Evaluation Factor

Do we have a program with great leverage?

- Is the need real?
- Is the rationale real?
- Is there a need/want?

Can the personnel be trained?

- Will the personnel be trained?

Is the plan real?
Is there a program idea (the art of the deal)?

- Can we develop it?
- Will it meet the need?
- Can we do it?
- Can our plan be competitive on design and performance?
    - On promotion to personnel and customers?

Is the price right?
Is the timing right?
Is it right in employee and customer presentation?
Can our plan be efficient in complete distribution of content?

- In management acceptance?
- In new development?
- In corporate marketing and promotions?
- In planned logistical and replenishment cycles?
- In other considerations?

Is it worthwhile?
Will it be profitable?
Can we afford it?
Is the R.O.I. and I.R.R. adequate?
Is the capital risk acceptable?

- Does it satisfy other company needs?
- Does it support company objectives?

Are external relations improved?

Is there an overriding factor?
Is our plan effective in defining the right I/T path?

- In enabling the core business processes?
- In facilitating management decision making?
- In growing the business?
- In improving the bottom line?

Have we defined our development environment?
Have we designed our corporate structure?

- Is it hierarchical?
- Is it horizontal?

Thought Break Two

Have you ever noticed that communication without passion is soon forgotten? Think about all the dull communicated visions you cannot remember. Better yet, have you ever seen leaders so passionate about their vision that they sell their passion but overlook their vision? These people just feel strongly about everything and may by chance have a vision.

Visions are not dreams however. They are much more complicated than wishful thinking. Since passion can infect an entire team and give it a life of its own, it is important for us to ramp up our critical thinking whenever we encounter the passionate vision of the inspired leader. Likewise, whenever we encounter the dull expression of a leader with the next great vision, we also should ramp up our intellectual horsepower and ask what is going on here? If the visionary is bored with the vision, chances are it is a boring vision, but it may be valuable. Stranger things have happened. Understand this: the passionless leader will not succeed in carrying the vision to reality. A passionless leader will require the passion of those on the team until eventually the team provides its own vision. In this case, the leader will become an echo in the memories of team members. Think about it.

4: Virtual Cybersecurity

Lately when reading the popular books that we all must read to remain proficient in our fields and disciplines, I have found myself wondering if I have been here before. I have witnessed the cycles from centralization to decentralization and back again, from growth to downsizing and back again, and from strategic planning to scenario setting and the death of strategic planning only to once again return to the importance of business capabilities as strategies. What have you witnessed?

Although many of us can easily find something common in these Change Management cycles, we all know by now that VC changed everything as it disrupted the competitive environment. Now this disruption escalates as VC enables commerce to become a virtual pursuit globally. This is the dawn of Virtual Commerce (VC) for sure. Obviously, it has transformed management thinking and management practice. Engaging 24X7 Virtual Commerce on a global scale demands an unfamiliar level of management dedication to vertical responsibility. It further demands a level of daring executive commitment to technology not required during previous business trends. With Virtual Commerce enabled by EC, executives can leverage their companies to become first, last, or in the middle of the competitive world. Where are you? If you do not lead your industry, and most companies do not, you should quickly become ready to change your life.

In the world of Virtual Commerce, executives can ill afford to maintain their usual leadership approaches. Many executives were forced to shift their traditional business priorities to achieving success in the world of VC. They had to rethink the fundamental Leadership question: Who do I work for? Is it the Board of Directors, stock holders, managers, customers, or the people who implement our business strategies? An incorrect answer risks time, money, personal and business relationships, and even careers.

At the core of Postmodern Leadership, answers may not be so obvious. Do we really understand what it takes to find new answers to old questions? I believe that we know more than we understand. But understanding is better. This is certainly the technological age as never before. Ready or not, leaders face a new reality: Today, every company is a technology company, big and small. Cyber Terror leads executives into unexplored territory.

While emerging Information Technologies change the rules of competition and the conduct of executive life., Cyber Terror injects a new level of worry and exhaustion. In answer to the common question that I so often hear in my seminars and engagements: We have not been here before. Competitively, strong Cybersecurity simultaneously demands both the unparalleled dedication of employees for a work environment that is both secure and safe. This is challenging because Virtual Commerce creates a transaction enabled environment in which business transactions occur so rapidly that errors mount incredibly fast, fast enough to produce a real Cybersecurity mess anywhere in the organization at any time in any core business process, secure or not.

In the world of VC, you can be first, last, or in the middle. Where are you when it comes to Cybersecurity? If you are first, good for you; if you are in the middle, I am happy for your involvement. However, if you are last, I must ask: Are you ready to change your life? If you wish to remain successful, you can ill afford to maintain current lifestyles. You must, and I do mean must, shift your leadership priorities and start thinking differently about who you work for and what you are risking. If you are a C-level executive, you better learn quite quickly what it takes to succeed with Cybersecurity in a Virtual Commerce driven world.

Cybersecurity in a Virtual environment offers a "Brave New World". It requires new answers to some old questions about you and your future, but from a radically new Systems Security perspective. Considering this, let me ask you a few direct questions, but as an executive competing in the 21st Century CYBER TERROR challenged environment. Table 3.0 below presents these important questions. If you cannot answer them, you need to get to work on Cybersecurity and connect with the executives already working on it.

Table 3.0: The Twelve Core Executive Cybersecurity Questions

1. Do you know what level of Cybersecurity you want for your company?
2. Do you know what level of Cybersecurity your colleagues want for your company?
3. Do you know what you want from the Virtual Commerce experience?
4. Do you know what level of Cybersecurity your company needs to remain safe and secure?
5. What do you want from others?
6. Do you understand why the business community advocates VC so radically?
7. Do you understand why you want to implement Cybersecurity to more safely engage in Virtual Commerce?
8. Why does your executive team resist or advocate the threat of CYBER TERROR? Why does your Information Services organization advocate its specific Cybersecurity approach?
9. Have you defined your Cybersecurity vision for the next few years?
10. Does it include Virtual Commerce as a framework for defining Cybersecurity in the enterprise?
11. Do you understand that other executives can answer these questions from different perspectives while working in the same organization?
12. Do you understand that you must work with them to agree upon and implement your Cybersecurity approach?

Since the management concern for Cybersecurity drastically changes the tens ions within the business environment, especially among the relationships which form this environment. The above questions, though truly basic, require deep thought. Even if you do not work on the Cybersecurity team, as you arrive at a reasonable answer to each question, you will find that whatever answers you come up with, your business success will depend on your success as a team builder resolving these 12 questions, especially a Cybersecurity team builder. To the team, you are the product anchor, the courageous visionary. For the team, you engage in many defining actions. This means that you establish the playing field and identify the windows of opportunity. You define competitors and isolate competitive leverage, and you select the strategies that your teams implement to assure that your Cybersecurity capabilities meet requirements.

Succeeding with Electronic Commerce

Commentators on E-Commerce, myself included, identify the dawn of e-commerce in the earliest attempts to develop Electronic Data Interchange back in the 1960's even before it became the Electronic Document Interchange that it is today (from data to documents). I can still remember working at the General Motors Dayton Data Center in Ohio and introducing the first ever very ambitious On-Line Regional Order Entry and Inventory Management System, termed FRONTIER, for the Frigidaire Division of GM.

The FRONTIER program was an early and complex attempt to engage in Virtual Commerce operations using computers, software applications, very large databases, and networks on a 24x7 basis. Although it was an Inventory Management System, it fueled the management desire to deliver real-time inventory management and product distribution capabilities to vendors throughout the country. True, several of the core applications consisted of tightly scheduled polling operations rather than continuous real-time business processes, nevertheless FRONTIER represents the initial commercial emergence of the fundamental beginning of Virtual Commerce driven business processes.

A number of v-commerce commentators have little awareness of these earlier v-commerce attempts. Such advances occurred, however, and led to many of the developments that we have today, even a few of those developments that commentators falsely believe are so recent. What a time that was, fun and games. I worked many long hours to support the roll-out of FRONTIER. Sadly, it was programs and projects like this that delivered the targets that Cyber Terrorists work so hard to disrupt. You see, CYBER TERRORISM is not new either. There have always been "bad actors" just as there have always been bad leaders.

Although the state of the art in hardware hindered the success of some of our early attempts at e-commerce, the creative environment existing back then encouraged the rapid mobilization of innovation and change. Fortunately, the requisite leadership, strategies, structures, and systems so conducive of progress in a technocratic world coalesced so nicely that the envelope of progress exploded throughout the last half of the 20th Century. Today, at the first quarter of the 21st Century, the prerequisites of progress in e-commerce remain very much the same. Leadership, strategy, structure, and systems are just as vital today as they were way back in the 1960's, perhaps even more so.

Today, the Cyber Terrorists who are hell bent on the destruction of their targets have trouble controlling their excitement. As Mark Antony put it so long ago, ""Cry 'Havoc!', and let slip the dogs of war". Good ole Antony, he sums up the mind of the modern CYBER TERRORIST quite well.

Virtual Commerce Leadership

Without mature and brilliant Leadership, Cybersecurity and V-commerce are eventually doomed. Nevertheless, executives at the pinnacle of decision-making commonly overlook the possibility that success with Cybersecurity requires the consistent commitment of themselves to making those very unpopular decisions that so many people complain about so often. It is all about the cost of "opportunity lost" if Cybersecurity failure occurs. If it becomes as bad as it could be, many people will be out of a job. No kidding. No exaggeration. CYBER TERRORISM is this serious.

If it is a public company that becomes disrupted, investors will be quite unhappy with the result. Leaders require courage to muster the will to make what could be eyepopping financial investments in Cybersecurity, to transform entire corporate cultures, and engage in competitive analyses at the strategic, tactical, and operational levels of their organizations on a continuous basis. Cybersecurity, just like Virtual Commerce, is not a short or temporary program. Cybersecurity is a permanent necessity for business success. Successful Cybersecurity requires wide-ranging intelligence, appropriate budgets, just the right mixture of people on the Cybersecurity teams, appropriately responsive technologies, continuous training and solutions adaptations, excellence in Behavioral Science Support, mature insight, the right blend of experience and reasoning, and other stuff I will not mention here, but some of you out there will know what I am not mentioning and why.

In today's competitive atmosphere, successful leaders have to be dedicated to the Cybersecurity of technology, data, and information with a heightened level of seriousness. Leaders require the self-motivation that ignites them to envision their internal and external Cybersecurity environments with a new expanded perspective. Moreover, success with Cybersecurity requires Leaders to connect (even aligning) strategies, tactics, projects, structures, processes, technologies, and systems with resources, visions, missions, and challenging profit expectations. Here, leaders now absolutely must learn to understand in-depth their company's state of readiness to form a mature Cybersecurity culture and realize the value of Cybersecurity every hidden corner of their companies.

Moving into the Cybersecurity Cosmos, leaders find begin to shift as they install new Cybersecurity structures, initiate relevant strategies, and implement more powerful Cybersecurity processes and system with human beings as components of such systems. Today, as never before, leaders become a component of their enterprise-wide cultures. In achieving the expected profitability, corporate leaders now must focus more on Cybersecurity design and acquisition, along with employee loyalty, costs reductions, optimization in channels of Cybersecurity introduction, and the identification of significantly impressive Insider Threat risks and mitigation than they do the management of old hierarchical teams and structures.

5: Leadership Strategy in the 21st Century

Once again business strategy has become unpopular. Systems Thinking and competitive disruption radically changed strategic planning. Indeed, Strategic Planning has completely evaporated in some sectors of business. However, even this emerged late in the game of business as many executives cannot distinguish between strategy, tactics, strategic planning, long-range planning, management philosophy, or the management approach. This situation leads to four definitive questions: What are they? What is the difference between them? Do you know how to articulate this difference? Where do you stand? While my experience has indicated that strategy has become a catch-all word used by a large number of leaders, I have found that in Cybersecurity, strategy is essential for success and refers to something specific, and often someone specific as in, "Bill! Call Helen. She knows what to do here."

In Virtual Commerce, strategy is tightly linked to the Internet-oriented value proposition and is here to stay. An appropriately designed Cybersecurity environment will make this possible. 21st Century strategy, including much of Cybersecurity, emerges from the core properties of the Internet and the behaviors of those who use it in more than a cursory way. While a number of executives still debate the enduing nature of the Internet, taking it to be a fad, believe it or not, many others have adopted it as a central business strategy.

Whether your vision has your organization moving toward full Cybersecurity integration, partial integration, or the integration only within specific business units, your organization faces the problem of developing Cybersecurity strategies that fit well with the overall goals of the larger corporate strategies. For example, you may need to integrate a special Cybersecurity intervention to develop and ensure a well-positioned online brand. Or, implement specific Cybersecurity (CS) systems and tactics to offer online-friendly products and services.

On the other hand, you may need to develop a new Cybersecurity organization simply to deliver high-levels of responsive Internet-oriented customer service. Or you may need to re-organize your Marketing and Sales organization to leverage cross-channel Cybersecurity coordination to improve customer acquisition. Whatever you do, you need to be sure that you are defining and implementing Cybersecurity (CS) strategies consistent with the vital interests and strategies of the corporate plan.

Have you hit upon a CS strategy appropriate to the business environment you find yourself entering at the first quarter of the 21st Century? For example, do you plan on becoming a pure-play Internet company or do you wish to remain a traditional brick and mortar operation heavily involved in Virtual Commerce? Whatever you decide, do you understand that today's business environment offers conflicting models of strategy in which the old so-called 7-S Model conflicts with the new? And do you realize that your CS solution is central to the success of whatever model of business you implement? Let me explain.

Executives based traditional business strategies on the old 7-S Model for sustaining competitive advantage (SCA). Executives generally know this. However, in today's business climate, characterized by the dynamic challenges of CS and an ever-changing business environment, the forces of hyper-competition have shattered past models of business competition. Until the last few years, executives forged a fit between their corporate strategies and the business environment in (1) structure, (2) strategy, (3) systems, (4) management style, (5) skills, (6) staff, and (7) super-ordinate goals. These seven aspects of strategic planning form the traditional 7-S framework for sustaining competitive advantage (SCA).

However, rather than seeking SCA, leaders of the new hypercompetitive environment seek disruption, even in legally daring ways. That's right, "Disruption". While SCA is a harvest strategy,

Disruption focuses on growth. In the view of the SCA folks, fit is crucial to business success. The SCA point-of-view attempts to cement a fit in four central domains of business competition: (1) cost/quality; (2) timing/know-how; (3) strongholds, and (4) deep pockets. Obviously, the drive for permanence guides the concept of strategic fit, even though such permanence is impossible. In the world of CS, permanence becomes an even a more challenging goal. Can you guess why?

Being a maintenance-oriented concept, executives derive the concept of strategic fit from the steady state model borrowed from physics and engineering. It is all very scientific, really? Differing from SCA somewhat, Disruption seeks the continuous evolution of new advantages. Does this include the affiliated evolution of Cybersecurity? While the SCA model ensures the predictability of company and competitor alike, Disruption throws out the rules and transforms every day into a new opportunity, or headache, depending on how well prepared one may be in facing such a brave new world.

Smart executives prepare for hyper-competition by adopting a new strategic approach in response to postmodern competition exhibited in the new 7-S Model which replaces the old 7 factors identified above: (1) superior stakeholder satisfaction; (2) strategic soothsaying; (3) speed in positioning for speed; (4) positioning for surprise; (5) shifting the rules of competition; (6) signaling strategic intent, and (7) simultaneous and sequential strategic thrusts.

In a hypercompetitive market, Virtual Commerce transforms growth into hyper-growth, the current size of a company being irrelevant. To achieve hyper-growth, follow the advice of Skip Weitzen and ask the right questions. Weitzen (1991) reminded us that failure occurs simply because management failed to ask the rights questions, the hard ones. He advised us to remain alert to windows of new opportunity. Every day really is new. The external business environment offers as many new opportunities as heart wrenching challenges.

Weitzen (1991) reminded us that anomalies are found in asking the questions someone else overlooked.

While companies must evolve to become great, truly insightful leaders form Evolutionary Guidance Systems (Banathy, 1987) to prepare their organizations for enduring greatness. This model includes Cyber Security as a subsystem of the HAS. Insightful leaders prepare themselves and their enterprises for growth, and so must you as a Leader. We all recognize that growth is challenging and difficult to manage. Everyone does well to become prepared to handle it. Weitzen urged us to "innovate then accelerate". Innovation and speed are the life blood of the postmodern business now required to include Cybersecurity as an essential subsystem. Competitive leaders use Information Technology to enable both. The necessity for Cybersecurity leads serious Leaders to rewrite the rules and re-define their ecosystems of business. Do not let your competitors define your ecosystem of business. Theya re happy to do it. Dominate and control as much of your competitive ecosystems as you can. You can leverage Cyber Security, business rules, and innovative technologies to grow. Today, business rules and innovative technologies alone are not enough.

Wishing to remain successful in the next century, great visionaries realize that 7-S management alone will not do it for them. Following Weitzen's (1991) insight, smart leaders also build new business models and apply the hyper-growth formula to the new 7-S framework outlined in Table 4.1 below.

Table 4. 1 Weitzen's Hypergrowth Success Formula

- Formula Description Component
- Anomaly: Find the overlooked or missed opportunity.
- Define the context of the emerging order in Metonymy which you and your enterprise will be operating.
- Discover the relationship between the anomaly, the inference, and the metonymy

- Expose products to those who influence product penetration preference.
- Stay ahead of the economic, social, political trends and techno-logical shifts that force rapid changes in Fads in your industry.
- Discovery: Continually seek new anomalies.
- Apply Weitzen's full formula: Anomaly + Computer Metonymy + Inference + Penetration + Trends and Fads + Discovery = Hyper-growth.
- Therefore: Hypercompetition + Success = Hypergrowth.

In a powerfully brief way, Weitzen identifies the basic elements of hyper-growth. Expanding upon Weitzen's wonderful insight by including the value of leadership, we obtain an enhanced view of the hyper-growth formula. This formula suggests that Vision 21® + Electronic Commerce = Virtual Commerce. Virtual Commerce + Capable Leadership = Hypergrowth.

While SCA places everyone on equal footing, hyper-competition pulls the rug out from under your feet. The disruption of hyper-competition forces executives to consider 21st Century strategies as they re-examine their worldviews. Hyper-competition reminds executives that although theory without practice is weak, practice without theory is a formula for failure

What is your corporate strategic theory, SCA or Disruption? Do you have a clear and simple mandate for executive practice and management actions suitable to Virtual Commerce? Finally, I ask you, do you really understand your new role in postmodern strategy innovation? Even if you serve as Chairperson of the Board, you report to someone who expects you to excel in strategic execution.

Few sovereigns rule in business. Business leaders operate in a world of constraints in which the expectations of others often dominate competition. Expectations may easily overwhelm us if we neglect to take care of business. Regardless of opinion, the expectations of the boss and customers pave the road to success. In the world of Virtual-Commerce, time waits for no one. Even though leaders may have only one chance to get it right, hidden agendas will nevertheless continue to do their damage. Beginning Virtual Commerce today, you should hit gold in about three years. But you must have what it takes to succeed and you need to initiate management practices more appropriate to 21st Century models of Virtual Commerce, and this means solid Cybersecurity or CS. Without CS, everything else becomes marginal, and day-to-day.

Cybersecurity Strategic Management

After corporate leaders have thrown their hats into the ring and made the decision to compete using virtual continuous strategies, 24/7, they proceeded to develop the appropriate Plans of Action. Not only did they educate themselves on the vexations of Virtual-Commerce, but they became more mindful about the intricacies of implementation. Now they find that this implementation model must absolutely include in-depth Cybersecurity.

In remaining successful with Virtual Commerce, management now realizes that it must transform their strategies into successful tactics assured by Cybersecurity. This means that management approaches traditional business and operational topics from an entirely new and broader perspective. For example, the practice of Multichanneling enters a new dimension with Cybersecurity. For example, the usual practices of brand management and naming, awareness, and association also take on a whole new look. So does the strategy of product selection, pricing, customizing, personalizing, and standardizing. Everything has become more complicated because everything now requires the constant protection of a well-designed Cybersecurity umbrella wherever possible. It is no longer a joke to claim that it is raining Cyber Security interventions.

Also, in Cybersecurity, Customer Service becomes daunting. Questions that challenge the use of personal instruction versus automated instruction are obvious, as are those regarding specific support mechanisms. How effectively can managers employ the new Cybersecurity strategies? Will managers go for common Cybersecurity solutions or opt out for something even more unique?

Management also needs to decide about the Bricks, Clicks, and Cyber Security question. How much of one or the other, all clicks and no bricks, or some beneficial mixture of each? Whatever is the choice, management then turns to the questions about applications of Cyber Security strategies for marketing and sales, supply-chain and manufacturing, retail versus wholesale, Human Resources, Research and Development, publishing, finance and accounting, and workflow management. Clearly, management makes a thousand and one decisions about the best way to leverage the new Cyber Security environment.

Cyber Security offers new opportunities for business process integration. These may offer a range of benefits in securing and maintaining control over the financial future possibly leveraging traditional advantages along with Cybersecurity, sharing critical business operational knowledge, coordinating vital strategies, and adjusting core competencies.

In Information Technologies, Cyber Security offers new opportunities for optimizing information management practices, verifying and managing Human Resources, capturing security and business measurements, and building improved customer relationships. Success requires management to continuously evaluate the organization's Information Technology capability, Cyber Security processes, Insider Threats, and capacities from within to remain ahead of the inflection point, i.e., that point at which the company loses its competitive position.

Cybersecurity and Corporate Structure

Cybersecurity significantly impacts the corporate structure. It requires new directions in internal investment and inside financing. It requires a new evaluation concerning the impact that the new Cybersecurity management practices may have on the commitment to separate business units. It may further require an assessment concerning the impact the integration of Cybersecurity teams may have on the building of Internet platform alliances. Implementing Cybersecurity strategies encourages new initiatives in outsourcing and well thought out strategic partnerships that enhance competitive posture.

In Management Systems, for example, leaders now must continually modernize internal business processes, implement incentive-laden human resources practices, align performance measures to attain realistic performance, and improve customer management. Cybersecurity includes many perspectives to protect the company. These move from the executive and strategic to the technical, end-user, and vendor perspectives. Cybersecurity processes also involve consumers, vendors, financial institutions, retailers, legal teams, and policy groups. No one is excluded. Since the principal reasons for adopting Cybersecurity practices are bottom-line and safety oriented, management will expect the organization to increase the speed and efficiency of transaction processes, enhance customer service, lower cost of operations, increase profit, while significantly reducing many yet unforeseen errors. These expectations will be represented in the new Cybersecurity performance measures. Cybersecurity will indeed challenge the "Bottom-Line" because it now has become a very expensive necessity. Security has always been a cost for many organizations. Now it has become a cost for everyone, company and customer alike.

6: Virtual Security Program

Management Environment

The mastery of the requisite strategies and structures of Cyber Security compels the responsible Leadership to develop and then implement a special Cyber Security Program Management Organization (CSPMO) to guide the enterprise through the often vexing and complex organization change processes emerging from the adoption of serious Cybersecurity support. The establishment of the CSPMO is necessary to politically facilitate the documentation, specification, staffing, implementation, and change processes constituting the new Cybersecurity environment. Since the scope of migration of a robust Cyber Security integration operation can be so daunting to some organizations, the carefully designed iterative approach offers significant advantages to maintain management control and corporate safety.

The enterprise-wide CSPMO functions as the hub of the Cyber Security Program. It reports to an executive steering committee composed of department heads and receives guidance and assistance from CS capable corporate audit and planning groups. The CSPMO also enjoys the services of appropriately qualified consultants as it directs, guides, and manages Cybersecurity implementation and management including CS for systems development, business process security maintenance, and operations management teams.

Cyber Security Design and Planning Process

I am not jesting when I say that documentation often defeats the program being documented. For the CSPMO, the unending questions, and there are indeed many, beg for answers. How much documentation is enough? Or, how much CS documentation is too little? We do not wish to overburden the enterprise with a mountain of documentation, nor do we wish to leave implementers in the lurch by not have something they really need at crucial times when documentation would make all the difference in the world for the success of the program. Counter-intuition plays a greater role in success than many people recognize. Experience is valuable when these questions arise.

For example, while it is true that some recognized companies have won notable awards for Quality by fully documenting everything, a few of these organizations have still managed to run themselves out of business, and all of this regardless of all the best documentation money could buy. While it still remains true that documentation is only documentation and the system is the process, the system requires documentation to be sensible and communicable to those who would implement, manage, maintain, and use it. However, we still have to ask: How much documentation is necessary? Believe it or not, this is a question of design.

The PMO and Design Inquiry

Design begins as an inquiry into the current and future situations. It is a look at the current status of the CS situation and where someone wants it to be right now and next year. CS Design Inquiry also implies the realization that the CSPMO is primarily concerned with the design and management of a special class of Human Activity Systems, i.e., systems in which the components are human beings. Let's face it; everything we do in the world is by, for, with, and through human beings. Design Inquiry is the same. It is about the design of a special type of Human Activity System dedicates to a special kind of service for human beings.

Design inquiry occurs conceptually at first. Engaging iterations referred to as the dynamics of design. Then the intellect proceeds through the spaces, systems, environments, and meta-systems of design. We can view Design Inquiry as an intellectual effort to create new security effective images of the future. It is a decision-oriented inquiry in that it seeks what should be.

Design is a common intellectual activity. It has been central to every human activity since the dawn of conceptual thought. Looking back in human history, we see that Marcus Vitruvius Polio made design a serious subject of inquiry as early as the First Century B.C. (Gasparski, 1984). Fast forwarding to the early 21st Century, we see that the design of the Virtual Secure organization has become a serious strategic and operational concern. Although re-engineering is the common expression everyone is so familiar with these days, the purest expression of the task of moving to Cyber Security is Design Inquiry. Even the expression re-design implies that someone employed design during the original development of the organization even prior to the introduction of Cyber Security. This, of course, may or may not be true. Some companies unfold on their own with little thought to their design. The seem to just "spring up" one day and then take off without much thought to design. Design is really the missing link in Cyber Security success. As mentioned above, Cybersecurity Design Inquiry occurs through the spaces, systems, environments, and meta-systems of Cybersecurity design.

Spaces of Cybersecurity Design

Cybersecurity Design stands as a cosmologically significant concept. Although some commentators such as Checkland (1981) see design as goals driven, Banathy (1984) reasoned that it is process oriented. For Banathy, design remains forever incomplete. Rooted in its own dynamics, design spirals towards a design horizon that infinitely moves away from the design's absolute attainment. Design, then, becomes an infinitely spiraling process in which its horizons forever retreat from its goals. Never reached, therefore, the designer can never realize the ultimate design destination.

Thus, we have an interesting Design Situation before us. Rather than formed in the desire to attain specific goals, the Cybersecurity Human Activity System (HAS) derives its magnetism from the excitement, force, and power of the Cybersecurity team's design vision. As the CS designers complete one aspect of their design, a new aspect to be designed emerges. For the CS design team, design is a "forever possibility". The CS team's design vision moves well beyond any temporal goal to establish an enduring repository of sought and possible goals. Therefore, the realization of CS design, although never achieved, is found in the qualitative longings of the CS designer for the highest accomplishment of CS innovation and implementation.

Lacking vision, design dissipates into the universe of mediocrity. Thus, CS design is constrained by mere goal attainment as executives who lack vision fail to build great CS organizations. In its most imaginative and powerful sense, design is a "Purposeful Human Activity". Moreover, we can see, therefore, that design compels change in the human universe. Here, CS designers use the power of the self-transcendent potential of the human person to guide the evolution of CS human systems emerging from the mechanisms of self-organization. Clear and simple right?

This is exactly what the Cybersecurity HAS delivers. Transcending Jones (1970), I prefer to say that with vision, design transforms the architecture of progress, the architecture of what is happening, and the architecture of being. This is exactly what Cybersecurity Human Activity Systems set out to do. They seek to guide the evolution of human systems emerging from the mechanisms of self-organization, and do it in a way that enables them to completely eliminate the treats and processes of CYBER TERROR.

Although goals are important to design and designers, they are not the entire design process. Rather, goals serve to assist designers in setting direction in design initiation. In design, goals provide targets but not destinations. Goals are the roadmaps, the rest stops, the temporal constraints, and the quantitative aspects of the Design Inquiry process. However, it is vision that gives meaning to the goals that generate the goals that replace current goals with new ones.

If CS Designers lack an appropriate vision, any goal will do. Understanding this, the designers of the Cyber Security HAS work to rapidly transform the architecture that enables the progress of Cyber Criminals as a dangerous HAS, the architecture that enables the Cyber

Terrorists to make progress, the architecture of what enables the Cyber Terrorists to do what they are doing now, and what they wish to do in the future. Emboldened by vision, executives engage in Design Inquiry within the appropriate conceptual spaces of design. We refer to these spaces as the:

- solution space;
- organized knowledge space;
- problem or contextual space, and
- experience space of design.

Design Solution Space

Working in this conceptual space, the designer identifies the purposes and goals of the design as milestones of the overarching design process. The interactive dynamics of design consisting of feedback and feedforward occur in this space. While the definition of the purpose of a human system initiates the design process, attaining the goals terminates only the initiation of the process. The Reproducer Subsystem functions in this space.

Knowledge Space

This conceptual space serves as the repository of the design process. It contains all the knowledge explored during design inquiry, including the specific, generic, and general design knowledge.

Problem or Contextual Space

This conceptual space contains all the sources employed in defining, studying, and characterizing all the problems, values and systems relevant to the CS design project (Banathy, 1984). The Contextual Space includes the environments and systems of cs design specific to the problem context and the existing Human Activity System or HAS. Meta-systems design and hyper-system definition occur in this design space.

Experience Space

This conceptual space is the design space in which CS designers test the alternative models against reality. The Experience Space includes the environments and systems of design specific to the knowledge base systems, the existing Human Activity Systems, the support systems, and the Design Inquiry system. Value systems design occurs in the experience space.

Systems of Design

The Design System engages in design. Technically, at a macro level the CSPMO is a Human Activity System that functions as an embedded project-oriented supra-system. More commonly, this system encapsulates all the others subsystems which form it. At the level of executive architecture, the CSPMO HAS itself consists of several subsystems including the Systems and Environments of Design. In all cases, the CS Design System interprets the design. While the subsystems vary in their detailed composition with each CS design project, generically they include: (1) System of Problems, Ideas or Intentions; (2) System to be Designed; (3) Design System; (4) System of Operations; (5) Knowledge System, and (6) Design Support System.

System of Problems

This conceptual system focuses on the problem context, including the existing problems in the existing HAS, such as the failure to define normative categories for Cyber Security strategy selection.

System to be Designed

This conceptual system focuses on the ideal system that is to be designed as the future Human Activity System.

Design System

This conceptual system produces the new CS HAS, i.e., Cybersecurity organization, in respect to the ideal CS systems models developed by the value system as a product of the meta-system. This HAS works in the domains of description, vocabulary, knowledge, and interpretations to engage in Cyber Security HAS design. The CS Design System conducts the Design Inquiry and interacts with the knowledge system to obtain knowledge about generating the action sequences of CS HAS design.

System of Operations

This system enables the operations required to initiate the Cyber Security Systems Methodology and plans and energizes the related systems in the Problem Solution Space.

Knowledge System

This system delivers all CS design process knowledge. This System delivers input to the Design System to energize the System of Operations within the Problem Solution space.

Design Support System

This conceptual HAS energizes the CS Design System using management and maintenance functions. This CS System empowers the CS Design System to manage the Design Inquiry and maintain itself as it designs the Ideal System.

Environments of Design

The systems of design do their job in the spaces of design. These in turn exist as the interfaces between the environments of design and the systems of design. The environments of design encapsulate each Cyber Sesurity Design System. They consist of the environments of the:

(1) System of Ideals-Aspirations-Intentions-Problems;

(2) Future System to Be Designed;

(3) Design Human Activity System, and

(4) Large Knowledge Environments derived from many different domains.

Environment of the System of Ideals/Problems

This conceptual environment represents the environment of the dynamic system of organizing perspectives. It consists of the ideas, aspirations, intentions, and problems that evolve into a new system.

This environment forms the conceptual space of the system of problems and consists of:

- the concrete, currently existing human activity system;
- a model of the new human activity system;
- the models of the objectives and goals of the new human activity system in the form of structural models;
- the system of intentions or values such as improved performance which ignited the idea to redesign the HAS.

Environment of the Future System

This environment serves as a conceptual source of inputs for the HAS to be designed, the new Virtual Commerce enterprise. This Environment contains the models of the future system and is the environment in which the new Human Activity System comes to reside.

Environment of the Design System

This environment cycles from the conceptual world to the physical. It provides all the matter, energy and information required for design. This Environment contains the design HAS and the models of the design system that will become a concrete system during design.

Knowledge Environment

This environment provides the inputs required to formulate the Knowledge Base System as an abstract system. This Environment is an abstract environment which contains the entire knowledge stock relevant to design as a disciplined inquiry (Banathy, 1984).

Meta-Systems of Design

Prior to beginning the design process, the CS enterprise designers engage in design inquiry to design the design project. Design inquiry is the design of design (Banathy, 1984), i.e., a Metadesign process. As meta-design, design inquiry identifies the meta-systems issues of design. "The particular system designed during problem definition and value system design is properly called a meta-system" (Hall, 1989, p.

97). Meta-systems emerge from decisions rather than conclusions. Designers base them on value judgments about the future system, that is, the system to be designed.

Designers use the facts and impressions about the problem situation to frame the system design problem. These lead to the first version of the meta-system. "A meta-system is a set of value sentences which describe the wanted physical system and imply or comprise the parts and relationships of the meta-system" (Hall, 1989, p. 97). Problem solvers employ value system design to evaluate design alternatives in arriving at the ideal system design.

During ideal systems design of the best possible system, we examine questions about formal, factual and value truth. Through value systems design, we construct meta-system models that will eventually become hyper-statements about the value and criteria for system selection from among the alternatives explored during design inquiry. These become the criteria of design selection and should fulfill specific system action requirements.

Value system design is normative design. It focuses on questions of ought and the relations between descriptive and normative system categories that describe the views of persons, workgroups, and HAS (Ivanov, 1990). We construct a hypersystem (Ivanov, 1990) to define, organize, and track the social relations examined during value systems or meta-systems design. Hyper-system design assists in value system design by framing the propositional categories requiring meta-system evaluation. Categorical relations of "Ought" judgments signify this system as a decision maker system, the client system

(Ivanov, 1990).

Interaction Dynamics in Design

As design activity flows among the environments, systems, and spaces of design, through the meta-system we engage in specialized interactions and dynamics that define the flow of the design process. During design, we do not engage in a linear activity consisting of discrete phases of analysis-synthesis and evaluation (Jones, 1963). Rather, as described by Banathy (1984), we engage in a process of interactive cycles characterized by the integration of the design dynamics.

Dynamics of Interactive and Spiralic Design

Here we progressively visit and revisit the conceptual spaces of CS Design until the new design of the human activity system emerges.

Dynamics of Feedback and Feedforward

Through these dynamics, we discern the iterative requirements of design. We go back and forth within the environments of design to discern the design requirements.

Dynamics of Divergence and Convergence

Searching for alternative CS designs, we settle on the most appropriate design for the goals and objectives of the Cyber Security (CS) design project. From Bogdanov (1984), systemic divergence tends towards evolution when design is influenced by complementary connections" (p. 133). Through conjunction, contra-differentiation produces quantitative equalization to reduce systemic contradictions as the system evolves. Bogdanov (1984) reasons, "convergence is the result of a similarly directed selection on the part of a similar environment" (p. 157).

Dynamics of Multi-Systemic Thrust in Design

Here we coordinate and refine preliminary CS designs throughout the design architecture to ensure that we consider every expediency of design.

Dynamics of Participative Design

We engage the exploratory and issues resolution cycles of design to ensure that we examine the relevant information of the design and listen to all comments. We engage in design as an iterative activity.

7: Designing the CSPMO Environment

Introduction

Now that we know more about the essence of Design Inquiry and the design process, we can begin to more effectively position the enterprise for its ascent into the Cyber Security universe. Doing this, the CSPMO focuses on the design of the planning and implementation Human Activity Systems as a continuum of the overall Design Inquiry from inception to realization. The CSPMO carefully documents these human systems throughout the entire continuum of design. Engaging the dynamics of design, the CSPMO iterates through the environments, spaces, and systems of design until the business, technology and implementation plans become realized as actual CSPMO deliverables.

The iterative planning process, resulting in the delivery of business, technology, and implementation plans, s essential to the success of the Cyber Security development program. Through planning, the CSPMO builds the repository of knowledge that guides the project teams through the iterations of program development.

Designing the Cyber Security Planning HAS

Planning is most often accomplished by a team that has come together for a common purpose. I view this collection of people a Human Activity System whenever it is characterized by the defining operations or processes of input, transformation, output, and feedback and adjustment. Typically for Cyber Security, the planning environment consists of the business, technology, and implementations Human Activity Systems and their environments. The CSPMO forms its meta-system of design by engaging in Design Inquiry to design the planning Human Activity System. The PMO uses the facts and impressions about the Cyber Security problem situation to frame the planning CSHAS design problem. During ideal systems design of the best possible Cyber Security HAS system, the CSPMO examines questions about formal, factual and value truth and uses these answers to identify CS planning milestones to be accomplished by the CS design system.

Working from the meta-system level, the CSPMO next begins to develop the separate planning environments by describing the environment of the CS design system to cycle from the conceptual world to the physical. It further designs the CS environment of the system of ideals, aspirations, intentions, and problems. The CSPMO ends design with the description of an acceptable CS environment of the future system as the conceptual source of inputs for the new Cyber Security enterprise. Working within the knowledge environment, the CSPMO describes the inputs required to formulate the Knowledge Base System as an abstract CS Human Activity System, the CSHAS.

Through the interaction dynamics in CS design, the CSPMO defines the flow of the CS design process. Here the CSPMO engages in the dynamics of interactive and spiralic design to progressively visit and revisit the conceptions described during CS design. In doing so, the CSPMO discovers the iterative requirements of design which become planning milestones. Along the way, through the dynamics of divergence and convergence, the CSPMO considers numerous alternatives which eventually lead to the most appropriate design solution. The CSPMO articulates this solution within the business, technology, and implementation of the CS development plans.

Working through the dynamics of multi-systemic thrust in design, the CSPMO coordinates and refines the preliminary designs composing the CS design architecture to consider each issue of Cyber Security impacting the ultimate CS design. From inception of the design inquiry, the CSPMO engages the dynamics of Participative Design to examine everything relevant to the design of the CS planning environment and to also consider all comments. Guided by the interaction dynamics of design to work through the environments, spaces, and systems of design, and using an appropriate meta-system methodology, the CSPMO documents the business, technology, and implementation plans with sufficient clarity to facilitate Cyber Security operations. To this extent, the plans address the issues found in each domain of interest, from business and technical to operational, and even financial and educational.

Cyber Security Business Plan

The CS business plan expresses the active vision and most probable mission of the company. It is a strategic document that considers the dual challenges of competition and the actual and immediate business situation. Although the CSPMO is interested in the company-wide business strategies, business process transformations, legal considerations, and questions of audits, TPAs, business continuity, budgets, cost and benefit tradeoffs, and the refined business case in respect to strategic positioning, it is most interested in the Human Activity Systems that makes all of these artifacts a reality through its very detailed and serious CS planning and implementation activities. This is not a game, but potentially is a make-or- break situation for an organization.

Technology Plan

The CS Technology Plan represents the technical extension or execution of the business plan. It represents a model of the technical architecture. This Plan links all technical plans with the strategic CS direction of the company. At an appropriate level of detail, this component of the business plan describes the cost of operations, technical, applications, workload capacities, and transaction architectures.

The Cyber Security Technology Plan further describes the Cyber Security, network, client, and systems interfaces, operational security, performance demands, and disaster recovery requirements, support environment, technical definitions, messaging protocols, project staffing, milestones and communications environment, as well as other aspects of CS and technical operations impacting the business plan and general corporate competitiveness.

Implementation Plan

With the business and technical plans, the CS design process delivers a model of the implementation plan that is linked to the business plan through the CS and business technical plans. This CS plan addresses the internal and external communications process and rules of engagement. It may include a pilot project plan or other cutover plan. It also details CS budgets, staffing, schedules, milestones, critical successes, Cyber Security stages, and failure factors.

This plan also includes project Quality Assurance and evaluation processes and procedures, conversion schedules, Virtual Commerce strategy initiation schedules, testing and acceptance procedures, production and maintenance plans, training plans, security rules and regulations, transaction processing roll-out schedules, audit and review plans, and sign-off and acceptance schedules. A useful implementation plan addresses, at the least, the training, communications, ramp-up, maintenance, Cyber Security, validation and acceptance, installation, and withdrawal stages of the CS programs. The following sections summarize the core activities that the CSPMO completes in making the transformation to an operational Cyber Security operation.

Prior to these milestones, however, the Cyber Security Program Management Office engages in Design Inquiry to make the conceptual leap from the current problem situation to the future solution. It does this while always remembering that the leap to Cyber Security involves the design of appropriate the Human Activity Systems required to build, implement, and maintain the new Cyber Security environment which itself is a Human Activity System.

Training

During the training cycle, the CSPMO conducts a thorough analysis of the situation. It obtains the necessary commitments and describes the internal challenges. The CSPMO also describes the internal audit, control, security, and quality requirements. The CSPMO further determines the costs and benefits of the program and documents all the expectations from the strategic to the operational levels of corporate engagement. Concurrently, the CSPMO targets the appropriate CS strategies, identifies the impacted business processes and determines potential pilot business partners. Finally, the CSPMO obtains the necessary and politically correct approvals from the business managers.

At this stage in the program, the CSPMO works with executives to determine the most appropriate strategic approaches to Cyber Security and to select the range of Cyber Security operations required to secure business operations. Prior to the beginning of transforming an enterprise into a Cyber Security oriented enterprise, visionary executives already know whether they will be a brick and click operation or primarily a click operation. They will also know whether they will include Cyber Security in sales, distribution, procurement, finance, or marketing and sales, or everywhere. Intelligent executives should have little trouble settling on a strategic approach.

To succeed with Cyber Security, executives find that they address a host of critical business issues concerning the regulatory and competitive environments, the significance of conflicts with existing strategies, as well as the problem of support, the depth of required commitment, and the confusion introduced by 24X7 Cyber Security operations.

Along with these concerns, training also addresses a range of legal and financial challenges impacting virtually every segment of Cyber Security and business operations from regulatory filing requirements to privacy and security to Trading Partner Relations. Management is expected to fully understand, and be clear on, the business opportunities, commitment requirements, critical success and failure factors, competitive risks, and the types and costs of necessary resources associated with the CS Program.

Training also reviews those critical internal issues that impact the adoption of Cyber Security. Cultural factors, staffing, trans-departmental relations, technology concerns, audit and control all impact Cyber Security success. Training also covers the types of prevention, detective, and corrective controls, and the costs, benefits and expectations of moving to the Cyber Security environment.

Communication

In this stage of Cyber Security implementation, the CSPMO completes and gains approval of the CS business security plans, finalizes, charters and publishes the CS strategic policy, establishes the CS program charter and communications process, commences management, staff, and client training, contacts and qualifies possible vendors, describes the new CS infrastructure, finalizes the various levels of the Trading Partner Agreements, and begins CS pilot program planning.

The various charters are crucial to establishing and empowering the Cyber Security Program Management Office (CSPMO) as the official CS task force. The CS Charter is a strategic document. It identifies the program sponsor and establishes the CS corporate direction, the business opportunity and business strategies, and key business objectives. The CS Charter should also identify the targeted business processes and their functions.

Program Preparation

Here the CSPMO describes the detailed Cyber Security operational strategies, and the transaction and business process protocols. The CSPMO also finalizes the CS information technology plans and implements the new Cyber Security infrastructure.

Pilot

During this stage, the CSPMO initiates the pilot project. The CSPMO organizes and prepares the team, charters the pilot process, finalizes all project plans, defines the security requirements of the CS pilot processes, and finalizes the acceptance protocols. Finally, the CSPMO finalizes sign-off procedures and criteria, obtains end-user agreement to customer acceptance details, and establishes final schedules and budgets.

Validation & Acceptance

The CSPMO commences pilot testing and conducts final acceptance testing. During the stage of Cyber Security cut-in, the CSPMO conducts post-pilot reviews, engages feedback and adjustments processes, publishes findings, implements required changes and adjustments, and prepares for full Cyber Security operations with targeted business partners.

Implementation & Withdrawal

The CSPMO makes necessary corrections to pilot design to finalize pilot program and cut it over to full prototype environment. The CSPMO updates and implements the CS rollout, commences the CS production operations and integrates maintenance processes. Next, the CSPMO announces program status with milestones results, commences the post-implementation review process, publishes the corporate-wide physical strategic plan for Cyber Security, refines external communications activities, and begins to expand Cyber Security capabilities. Finally, the CSPMO cautiously withdrawals from active development of this cycle of Cyber Security activity and proceeds to new Cyber Security cycles.

It is not so much the planning documents that are so important; it is the knowledge attained through the planning process that enables the CSPMO to successfully execute its programs.

8: The CIO & the BIG

New Business Relations

If you are an executive sponsor of the Cyber Security operation, your success will remain elusive unless your organization nurtures a solid Business Intelligence Group (BIG) that reflects your own vision, political skill, professional confidence, and success. As a C-level executive, you are expected to be a visionary. As a visionary, your company only succeeds if your vision succeeds. If you fail, all fail. Paradoxically, Visionary Rule Number One: You succeed only if your people succeed. Successful executives work for their people. They deliver the direction and resources that their people need to do their jobs.

Inspiring the Business Intelligence Group (BIG) Challenges21st Century executives are expected to master new skills. So, what's new? Foremost among these, is mobilizing others to succeed. Leaders lead, even when they have to defer to others. If you desire to lead the BIG in your enterprise, you can start by influencing the social art of change. Cyber Security requires a significant change in attitudes about security and safety. Moreover, people expect CS leaders to rationally determine their CS wants and needs for the enterprise based on detailed intelligence of the current and anticipated future situations.

The CSPMO expresses its vision of possible CS futures while always anticipating outcomes for various scenarios. IT is a good thing to remember that it is the secure who are the humblest among us. Insecurity will defeat our noblest aspirations. Finally, the CSPMO does well when it respects and supports the emerging roles of Chief Enterprise Architect and Chief Information Officer (CIO). The success of both of these positions directly depends on the success of the Cyber Security organization just as the success of the Cyber Security organization depends on the success of the Chief Enterprise Architect and the Chief Information Officer.

Management Information Systems is dead. In the 21st Century, the most senior executive, whether President or CEO, looks to the

Chief Intelligence Officer to manage the information and business intelligence flows of the enterprise. In post 20th Century managerial wisdom, the Enterprise Intelligence Officer (EIO) becomes the enterprise ecologist who carefully examines strategic consequences of Cyber Security by skillfully identifying underlying phenomena which inform executive strategic action via scenario setting. In this sense, then, the EIO works with the Chief Executive Officer to replace forecasting with Cyber Security scenario setting as an appropriate response to the new environments introduced through Virtual Commerce, protected through Cyber Security, and implemented through Electronic Commerce, which seems to be a continuous process of never-ending transactions.

The Enterprise Architect has an evolving role that demands serious attention. As the business environment changes, so too did the role of the traditional MIS Director. With the increasingly strategic and operational roles of Information Technology in the human environment, the EIO is expected to design strategic information flows to support the business plan. The EIO complements the traditional activities of MIS by adding engaging strategic support, which includes in-depth Cyber Security.

As one of the top five corporate executives, the EIO partners with the Chief Executive Officer to empower, not only enable, secure business operations. Assisting the Chief Executive Officer in this capacity, the EIO further assists in defining the business security vision by identifying core security values and related goals for future business success. It is the role of the EIO to employ a secure Information Technology to leverage the corporate and team Cyber Security values and goals. In the expanded role of strategic business executive, the EIO establishes the vital security strategies that enable the company to attain its goals. Thus, the EIO sets the Cyber Security performance milestones as targets to enable the organization to securely achieve those goals. Moreover, as the chief enterprise technologists, the EIO employs the mechanisms and technologies of the Information Age to transform the business and security visions into operational practice.

Departing from predecessors in Management Information Systems, the EIO now focuses on business rather than only technical issues. Strategic Cyber Security envisioning, designing core security and business processes, and empowering the productivity of each business process become the fundamental concerns of the EIO who now must go the extra mile to clarify the relationships between business processes, Information Technology, Cyber Security and business partners.

Success is elusive for the postmodern EIO whose tenure lasts around two years or less. The successful EIO defines the scope and purpose of Cyber Security and technology in the strategic organization while ensuring that the BIG supports business goals. The EIO implements Cyber Security standards, guidelines, and policies to securely leverage technology for business success. The EIO also ensures that Information Technology improves the bottom line or generates new lines of business opportunity. Also, the EIO clarifies the rationale for employing Cyber Security technology in specific ways that satisfy the detailed expectations of end-users and customers for secure process improvement.

Meeting emerging demands, the EIO employs technology as a strategic resource and tactical tool. Operationally, the EIO applies design science to solve business problems and, depending on the model adopted, leads enterprise-wide efforts to optimize business performance through enhanced Cyber Security operations. Thus, the EIO establishes standards to integrate technology and Cyber Security into the executive agenda of improved business performance and profitable growth. Scaling responsibility and opportunity, the EIO brings deep and broad experience to the executive team to facilitate the success of business plans. The EIO unifies the strategic, tactical, security, and operational thrust of business into a unified program of action. In this way, the EIO designs new models of effective business practices and introduces new approaches of secure information movement and management to unify the business environment.

For the enterprise, the EIO solidifies new business relationships with vendors, customers, distributors, and agencies via the design of improved Cyber Security architectures that enhance the security of Electronic Commerce, EFT, and so forth. Here, the EIOs may fail unless they partner with other senior executives to identify core areas of business opportunity such as highly secure and powerful order generation and fulfillment processes. This approach was a key to success at Dell Technologies.

The EIO empowers the enterprise by optimizing the interfaces between business and technical systems and employing strategic information processes. First and foremost, the EIO designs effective security and technology architectures that empower, not only enable, business processes. Going beyond the role of MIS Director, the EIO designs enterprise-wide highly secure business architectures and introduces technology into the component workflows.

Making the necessary impact, the EIO is expert in enterprise change methodologies and is an adept designer of 21st Century business architectures. Moreover, the EIO understands the information flows of core business processes and knows how to employ methodologies to link the appropriate performance measures of business practice with Cyber Security. The EIO integrates Configuration Management approaches with New Product Development processes. The BIG responds by building enterprise models of secure business structures and processes rather than models of Information Technology and client environments.

21st Century Enterprise Information Officers are experienced and knowledgeable. They possess notable experience in the three trusts of planning as well as the design of progressive business models. Additionally, they are masters of both horizontal and vertical management practices. They excel at hypercompetition and can implement both the sustaining and disruptive models of competition. The EIO delivers seasoned leadership skills as they bring a strong record of success to Executive Management through the implementation of Information Technology. If you are wondering what you must do to succeed as an EIO, you can adopt several of the personal strategies outlined in Table 7.1 below.

Table 7. 1 Strategies for Succeeding as an
Enterprise Information Officer

1. Clarify the difference between your personal goals and those of your company.
2. Become a self-motivator empowering yourself from the inside out.
3. Maintain high levels of personal integrity when involved in political engagements.
4. Make change a team effort
5. Become a real partner to all end-users and customers.
6. Obtain success by working with cross-functional teams.
7. Nurture positive relationships everywhere.
8. Define new rules for ensuring success.
9. Grow carefully by achieving small successes.
10. Regularly review your personal history while changing your mind, opinions, and past approaches if appropriate.
11. Prepare for the future by giving others an out.
12. Never seek or expect appreciation.
13. Accept the differences of others while focusing on their 13. strong points.
14. Develop an action plan for leading change focused on real 14. growth.
15. Value your expertise and share it carefully.
16. Innovate everywhere.
17. Identify the most important problems facing your 17.

company.

18. Prioritize alternative solutions.
19. Recommend appropriate management actions.
20. Solicit the ideas of those above you and listen.
21. Act on the decisions of management and the conclusions of executives.
22. Model your expectations from the business rather than 22. technical perspective.
23. Respect and earn the respect of your boss.
24. Work by priorities only.
25. Set performance records by doing more with less; you are 25. competing in the business Olympics.
26. Apply your vision and values consistently.
27. Be a courageous risk taker and lead the BIG.
28. Reward yourself while continuously shaping and 28. reshaping your role.
29. Develop an action plan for leading change focused on real growth.

In an e-commerce environment, the EIOs become masters of the cross-functional enterprise. They had better talk the talk and walk the talk. Since EIOs work for their people and report upward, they should do everything in their power to make a difference to their employers. Because the forces of global competition make dinosaur brained leadership ever more insufficient in today's business climate, the EIO's leadership skills become a core corporate asset. Smart EIOs nurture and develop their leadership acumen with great wisdom.

Enterprise is about leadership. But leadership does not just materialize out of thin air. It requires understanding, courage, single mindedness, drive, followership, and an ability to negotiate, persuade, motivate, encourage, and influence others. If your company runs short of capital, it can borrow it. But if your organization comes up short on leadership, it will have little chance of surviving.

"Nobody doubted his capacity to rule until he became emperor,"
(Tacitus on Galba).

"I believe that the principal reason why some firms survive, prosper and expand, while others dwindle, perish or sell out, must be sought in the personalities of the men and women who manage them," (Charles Wilson).

Guided by an in-depth and noble vision, the Business Intelligence Group links the facts of business performance to the wisdom of executive experience to mold strategic conceptualizations and inform executive conclusions.

9: The Transition from Manager to Leader

A number of EIOs earned their wings as technical managers. Occasionally, these humble beginnings create more problems than they solved since the technical view differs considerably from the business view. For one thing, business leaders generally recognize that they exist to provide better products and services to customers at a profit in a cutthroat environment offering little loyalties. The technologies required to facilitate this process usually take second stage to the business process. On the other hand, a number of MIS Directors ascended the ranks of the corporate dream-world by artfully selling their Information Technology plans to business leaders. While MIS people thrived on state-of-the-art technologies, an enterprise may go belly up if executives suspend sound business judgment in favor of the latest Information Technology innovation.

The world of the EIO markedly differs from that of the MIS Director or the CIO. Although the transition from CIO to EIO challenges the less prepared, it works well for the EIO who has nurtured a well-informed business perspective. Professional success requires the EIO to become adept at juggling many competing leadership challenges. The best EIOs have mastered the art of controlling their lives by proportioning their time among executives, managers, staff, customers, and themselves. These EIOs leverage their time in two important areas: (1) Focusing on the essentials of the job, and (2) consistently pursuing their continuous Intellectual, emotional, and professional development. Not only is the EIO expected to manage upward by participating in endless executive team

meetings, but (s)he also manages vertically to guide the BIG in anticipating and responding to the changing demands of business competition

Following the EIO's move up the corporate ladder, everything changes as the familiar presuppositions of management go out the window. Reality is the harsher sister of ambition. Now the project approval process assumes a different dimension as the new EIO learns that executives negotiate an entirely new set of rewards on an up-front and personal basis. As senior executives, CIOs now must find their personal fulfillment in their governing values. EIOs are core enterprise leaders after all. They suffer the folly of children when they do not know their governing values. When their daily activities reflect their governing values, EIOs enjoy inner peace. It is this inner peace that delivers all real success. Like the rest of us, the behavior of EIOs' reflects their true beliefs. What they love is who they are. EIOs satisfy their needs when they become consistent in thought and action and work hard to ensure that their beliefs become consistent with reality.

EIOs can overcome their self-defeating behaviors if and only if they are willing to change their incorrect beliefs. Although this is certainly easier said than done, EIOs can engage in a therapeutic process termed re-decision to weed out unnecessary emotional and intellectual baggage. The EIO quickly learns that executive self-esteem ultimately comes from within, not from the job, nor the boss.

As C-level executives, EIOs remain cautious about the political nature of their executive relationships and look more to oneself to affirm their success by meeting business goals and affirming corporate success. An authentic senior executive never depends on the judgment of others to know how she or he is doing. Such forms of approval seeking may indeed mask a deeper problem of emotional dependency and insecurity. Rather, mature EIOs ignore approval seeking behaviors altogether in favor of reading the signs of the process, as opposed to depending on the contextual level of communications.

Unlike their subordinates, EIOs enjoy very different comfort zones.

Personally, I maintain that if you do not enjoy change and the challenge that insecurity at the top brings, you should avoid the promotion to EIO. If you have enjoyed a significant tenure with your company, you had better be prepared to kiss it all good-bye when you move up. The odds dictate that you will soon be moving out.

"Up and out," is the motto of the EIO. As mentioned above, the average length of service of the EIO is less than two years when you factor out the MIS Directors and DP Managers. Obviously, to achieve any significant goal, EIOs modify their comfort zones and accomplish much in a shorter time. Basically, EIOs become very good at what they do. Merely to have a chance at winning the political game, they must develop enough of a staff following to make a difference.

What all of this means may not be so easy to grasp. After all, no one is impervious to error, and we all have something to work on in one way or another for most of our lives. It does mean, however, that if the executive must lead, (s)he will never lead. If the EIO gives more, the EIO will have more. EIOs become successful by sharing success. More to the point, the successful EIO has learned to overcome the following five myths of management.

First, contrary to popular wisdom, the boss really does not control the organization. More often than not, external forces control the boss. More than one boss has uttered: There go my people; now I must find out where they are going so that I can lead them.

Second, consultants cannot save anyone from anything. They are not messiahs. More often than not, consultants generate solutions that lead to even greater problems down-stream. More than one consultant has uttered: This year's solution will be next year's problem.

Third, contrary to the common wisdom of this age, not all organizations can succeed even if their products or service make sense. If you offer an acceptable product and can deliver, you have what it takes, but only if you commit to success. More often than not, organizations achieve success because of intrinsic factors that go beyond products or service. More than one organization has uttered: Our products were the best and our service was excellent, but our timing was lousy and our credibility disappeared.

Fourth, if you are an EIO, it is an error to believe that technology will solve all the problems. Technology creates problems faster than solutions. Give a weak employee a computer and you end up with a weak employee with a computer. Apply a computer to a weak business process and you end up with weak business process with a computer. This year's system is next year's problem. More often than not, EIOs taste the bitter salt of disappointment because they failed to make the leap from technology manager to business visionary. More than one EIO has uttered: I thought that it was strategic common sense that the company should spend more money on computer operations than on marketing and sales operations.

Fifth, you are living a myth if you believe that there is one best way to manage. If you believe this, you are not a systems thinker. There are good ways and bad ways to manage. Some ways may even be more appropriate than others. But given the diversity of the human intellect and the richness of human history, there is no best way to manage. More often than not, managers who believe that there is one best way to do things only know one way to do things. More than one manager has uttered: I thought my way was the best way. Little did I know that it was the best way to reaching the unemployment line.

I am not smart enough to know the best way to do anything.

10: A CHANGING WORLD

A Changing Constant

Both philosophers were correct: Nothing under the sun is new, and everything is in flux. So much for Heraclitus! The only constant in life is change. Not wishing to splash anyone's river, I suspect that this paradox is nowhere more meaningful than in the life of the executive. If we consider the shifts in management thinking over the last 25 to 30 years, including the change in perspective from function to process, a picture of the cyclic nature of the executive environment emerges. Truly, nothing under the sun is new and everything is in flux. The fluid nature of the business environment significantly contributes to the complexity of executive life.

Over the last few years, consultants have bombarded executives with countless management themes ranging from speed, quality, and productivity to profitability, earnings per share, and customer service. Important strategies calibrated to these themes of value proposition have included the re-engineering with quality craze and the market traction group. As the fallout from these themes emerges, and Boards demand that executives fix even worse messes, pundits announce a new round of solutions to sustain competitive advantage, as if such a goal is possible.

Themes and movements currently advocated by management consultants include the death of strategic planning, innovation, flexible manufacturing, rapid response, resilient management, information as an asset, shrinking to grow, holonomic-based management, vertical management, dynamic architecture, dynamic planning, continuous benchmarking for best practices, values enrichment, management by values, speed as an asset, the management wave, enlightened leadership, simplicity, reframing organization, business ecology, enterprise alignment, disruption, and on and on.

If executives think that they must adopt one of these themes to survive, they will find that survival will likewise become problematic. The question that keeps haunting me is this: As a prerequisite to managerial success, how do executives arise to the pinnacle of decision making without first expanding their skills as consultants? Indeed, even though many consultants have never held an executive position, this fact does not deter many of them from having all the answers. Sometimes I wonder who should be consulting to whom? What in the world is going on here anyway? What came first, the consultant or the business executive? Forget the chicken and the egg, this is the real paradox. To better understand my sarcasm here, you might take a moment to contemplate the information in the following Thought Break.

Thought Break Three

About 20 years ago, a new CEO and entrepreneur invited me to his company to tour its modern business complex. Yes, it was certainly an impressive setup, and very expensive. He spared no cost. When I asked him who his best customer was, he replied that he did not have a customer yet, the business was too new. Nevertheless, he reminded that he had a great company!

With interest, I naturally asked him what made his company so great. With all the enthusiasm in the world, he replied that he advocated all the latest management techniques, attended all of the best motivation seminars, including the power seminar of Anthony Robbins, and placed a computer on every desk. He could not fail he argued because he was well up on the latest success portfolio of management approaches and definitions of leadership. When I asked about his plan for growth, like getting his first customer, he replied that he was buying a marketing plan from a consultant. With this he planned to teach his sales staff how to convince his future customers to buy the services he intended to offer, which, by the way, was consulting on personal marketing success. I am not making this up, no kidding.

After all of this, he asked for feedback. My reply was to the point: You are not in business until you have a customer. Consulting advice, marketing plans, tremendous buildings, powerful computers, and high levels of personal motivation bolstered with encyclopedic knowledge alone never make one successful in business. I do not deny the importance of these factors in building business success. At critical times all such ingredients of management success can and sometimes do help. However, the record is clear. Even with all of these advantages, a great number of businesses still fail while others without them still manage to succeed.

When I asked about his deep and noble vision for his business, he replied that this vision nonsense is just a bunch of nothing. Anyone can dream up a vision in a second. Thinking about visions only wastes time. What an insightful revelation I exclaimed. His vision was that vision does not matter. Visions did the matter to him.

I guess he did not understand the reasoning behind his own argument. He had just announced that he did not know why he became an entrepreneur, but it does not matter. I guess that without realizing it, he agrees with the radical behaviorist and evolutionary materialist who argue that all human history would be exactly the same even if human beings never had a thought at all. A vision, therefore, as an artifact of thinking, must be an epiphenomenon of executive success.

What irony! Is it not interesting that many of the proponents of these modern themes of management thinking have never personally experienced life as a C-level executive? I have found that executives generally excel at what they do; this is how they got to be where they are. Personally, I do not believe that successful people would be any more successful by taking advice from me. Insight not advice is the game of advantage. Newkirk's Law #13: "If you must study business to be in business, you have no business being in business." Success in business involves a deeply personal experience. A business vision signifies a personal commitment to success in life and business. An in-depth and noble personal vision for business success is not trivia. All success flows from it.

I cannot but help wonder if so much change and fashion actually occur in business because of executive fear? So many people forget that the principles of business success are basic: The business person provides a product, and a service is a product, to a customer who pays for it. Presto, it is as simple as this and has been for thousands of years. Here is the beginning of business: I sell, you buy. Sometimes, nothing can make this happen good enough. My colleague Gene Kerfoot would tell me that "good enough" is really good enough. Everything else is counter-productive. I would always ask myself: "How much good is required to be good enough"? I suppose the answer depends on how good an executive is at being an executive.

Business success is a deeply personal experience beginning with the psychology of vision. Regardless of your fear over who is at your heels, who you hire to work with you, or what trend you buy into, business success will forever remain elusive. Fundamentally, your product or service has to be sensible to the customer from many different perspectives. It is good to remember that marketing consultants offer marketing plans not business success, computer consultants offer technical consulting not business success, and outplacement firms offer job search techniques not personal success.

I am not saying that consultants and their themes have no value. I am a consulting specialist. I coach other consultants to facilitate the problem solving of their clients. What is most important is how clients use the consultants they hire. I think experienced consultants are excellent for sharing insight and solutions. When engaged properly, consultants may enable clients to rediscover the road to success. One should understand, however, that consultants remain meaningless if clients fail to offer a noble in-depth vision for mobilizing innovation and change to achieve success.

Ironically, many of the themes of current consulting practice originated in the death pains of failing companies, not successful ones. What good is a best practices benchmark if the standard it defines originated in mediocrity? Best practices allow us to be good followers. Thus, we can be no worse than anyone else, safe but not great. Think about it.

11: Changing Role: Evolutionary Guidance

The Only Leadership Role

Have you ever attempted to describe the role of Chief Executive Officer (CEO) to a group of consultants, and I do mean group? Do you remember how frustrated you became whenever each consultant obnoxiously pointed out all the exceptions to your explanation? They all know someone who does not fit the mold.

What mold? Some CEOs travel constantly and seem to live by speeches primarily serving as public relations officers. Others engage in functional duties. Still others provide staff support. Others like Chainsaw Al specialize in one program of staff cutting after another while reserving all the credit for innovation. Not much innovation here. Others remain in the background and keep their approaches to themselves until their Boards have had enough. It is no joke when I say that the job description of your neighborhood CEO is all over the place.

Some of these individuals take the easy road. Rather than face each situation as a unique opportunity for creativity, a few business leaders merely use a formula for downsizing, or outsourcing, and continue from there while perhaps unnecessarily shattering thousands of lives. Who knows what the others do? Often I hear CEOs remark that they do not have a clue what other CEOs do. Not too surprisingly, I also hear others comment that they have no idea what their CEOs know or how they got to the pinnacle chair. I most often hear this from the small number of remaining middle managers after the bloodletting has paused.

Shrink to be great is their motto. For many managers and CEOs, the role of the CEO remains difficult to define. The question has merit: What does the Chief Executive Officer do? My research indicates that we do not yet have a generally accepted answer. By the time an answer emerges, the role of the CEO will doubtlessly change. Not only is the business environment continually in flux, so too is the role of the

CEO who can never walk into the same company twice, as Heraclitus suggests.

Earlier, I spoke of executive fear that characterizes today's business environment. Fear may be an unfair characterization, but probably describes the real situation. Executives face a daunting challenge. If the CEO succeeds, and is a good negotiator, she or he increases self-confidence and gains the prestige and material rewards that business success at the pinnacle brings. If CEOs fail, they question their self-worth and wonder about the material rewards that might have been or may yet be at the next company.

As in every other century, CEOs earn their success; it is never freely realized. Life in general blends many unknowns and inevitably becomes a symphony of separation as one generation gives way to the next. Moreover, many of an executive's best management techniques emerge from a mixture of informed wishful thinking bolstered by a keen intuition born of seasoned experience. Hope really is not a strategy even though executives are driven more by emotion than intellect as they continually go into undiscovered county. Every day is really a new day.

The journey to business success often leads executives to visit new territory as many problems have no reference to solutions from the past. Like everyone else on this globe, CEOs are future living but backward thinking, as Nietzsche put it. Business success develops from the blend of many tangible and intangible ingredients. Timing, innovation, pricing, aesthetics, product, mistake, competitor anomaly, quality, demand, knowledge, skill, apparent luck, experience, resources, psychology, and the unknown all contribute to business success.

Competitive fear produces that humbling sensation arising whenever executives realize that many things will forever remain beyond their control. Yet the buck stops with them. While a few CEOs believe their own hype and never learn the lesson of fear until they ultimately fail, many recognize their shortcomings and endeavor to overcome them. The more experienced CEOs further understand that a one-time success regardless of magnitude does not guarantee a record of success. Business success remains fleeting for most CEOs. Only a few ever make it to the summit of recognition. Paradoxically, success is the prerequisite to failure.

In my lifetime, Elon Musk, Bill Gates, Donald Trump, Michael Dell, Ted Turner, and Ross Perot have few peers and their stories continue as an unfinished drama. For them, in company with the rest of us, failure ever looms over the horizon as a reminder of the human capability for error. Bill Gates gained the opportunity by virtue of circumstances not all of his making. However, he was where he needed to be when the right situation developed. Additionally, he had the foresight and the in-depth vision to commit. The rest is history. Ross Perot also ensured that he placed himself where he needed to be at the right time. He also had the noble, in-depth vision to commit. He acted and the rest is history. Michael Dell carved out a little different personal history. However, all three of these great people leveraged anomaly to succeed. Donald Trump and Ted Turner also worked hard to overcome challenges that would sink most CEOs. Without their unique visions, however, history would tell a very different story about every one of these men.

Complex psychological forces occasionally mute the gilded record of success of many a CEO into a one-time tragedy as success itself becomes the road to later failure and even humiliation. Consider the executive record at Apple Computers over its history. What a roller-coaster! Or, look at General Motors and Ford only a few years ago. Talk about being out of touch with a loyal market. Let others build the hybrids, it will only amount to an insignificant share of the market not worth pursuing. I knew a COO of a prominent company who told me back in 1999 that the Internet is only a fad and will disappear soon. Wow!

In one of the most interesting paradoxes of life, success often breeds failure in both business and life. Although the general principle is correct that we learn better from success than failure, and success breeds success, we can make a case that for those at the pinnacle of decision making, success also breeds failure. The early Romans understood this principle all

too well: "Thou art just a mortal man."

Ironically the slogan "if it is not broken, break it" offers valuable insight. A CEO believing one's own press, becoming complacent or satisfied with the status quo, capitulates to a formula for failure. The competitive nature of business brutalizes the Olympics of Commerce. Once you enter the event, you must continually do your best. In the competitive environment of the business Olympics, CEOs become star athletes while consultants serve as the trainers, coaches, or motivational managers who may or may not have been a CEO earlier.

Indirectly, the executive consultant defines and redefines the role of the CEO. As new trends and insights emerge, consultants assist CEOs in the transition to new models of executive leadership. Moreover, as a CEO works with other executives, a Human Activity System (HAS) emerges composed of about a dozen value specific dimensions. Human Activity Systems are systems in which the components are human beings.

This executive level HAS directs the enterprise to adapt to challenges and opportunities in the environment and continually shapes the internal values of the corporate culture. The Evolutionary Guidance System (EGS) framework offers a powerful model for guiding this executive system. Banathy (1987a) identifies the EGS dimensions as the aesthetic, economic, educational, ethical, political, scientific, social action and technological. Evolutionary Guidance Systems are idealized or value systems. Collen (1990) writes: "When a HAS commands the direction of its own activities, activities which serve to guide it in the pursuit of its mission, the HAS seeks to become an EGS"

(p. 8).

The executive level EGS as an idealized Human Activity System performs three defining functions. First it establishes an organizing perspective to inspire executive leadership. Second, it defines idealized goals for core business processes. Third, it provides a framework for designing the ideal business processes as a guiding notion for the new work environment. Ideal business processes derived from a particular EGS describe an idealized enterprise model which becomes the new benchmark for evaluating all work performed by the core business processes.

Through loops of feedback and adjustment, the idealized model guides the business processes to both:

- Meet the business requirements of the company, and
- Attain their own goals.

Evolutionary Guidance Systems share many of the attributes of appreciative systems. Sir Geoffrey Vickers (1983) described an appreciative system as a dynamic, personal and social work of art sharing three defining attributes.

- First, it corresponds with reality enough to guide action.
- Second, it is shared enough by others to mediate communications.
- Third, it becomes acceptable by ourselves to make life bearable.

Peter Checkland (1986) views appreciative systems as interacting processes of continuous ideas and events which continually unfold. They transcend themselves by critically reflecting on their past.

As an Appreciative System, the EGS shares four central traits: (1) Holistic view of organizations as they co-evolve with the environment; (2) the value of the appreciation of individuals and local communities as an ethical foundation; (3) social network of co-operative learning, and (4) ecological axioms of strategic, tactical, and operational significance.

In the personal domain, the Appreciate EGS advocates: (1) Self-awareness and self-management; (2) respect for elected relationships; (3) associative level of work and career relationships, and (4) obligation of involvement as a world citizen. Interestingly enough, a few leaders view these traits as controversial. Can you guess why?

CEOs employ the appreciative EGS model to inspire an enterprise to meet environmental challenges and shape the internal values of the corporate culture. Guided by the EGS model, executives succeed in the future by capitalizing on realistic opportunities as the EGS provides guiding principles of effective management practice such as diversity, optimization, cooperation, self-regulation, transformative change, connectedness, equivalence, and learning from experience.

The Appreciative EGS model describes the new role of the 21st Century executive team as one of evolutionary guidance. This model provides an effective approach for succeeding with Virtual Commerce by formalizing the role of appreciation in business, appreciation of employees, customers, society, and the environment, and doing something about it in the course of business competition.

Rapidly attaining business leverage, executives employ their own unique visions to integrate Information Technology with strategic action. In spelling out the most effective road to enterprise progress, the unique executive visions provide more than a predetermined plan of uncritical assumptions. Informed by the appreciative EGS model, the unique executive visions guide the evolutionary unfolding of an enterprise to attain significant levels of success. As an example of the power of the EGS model, future chapters describe how we designed the Systems Management Institute as an appreciative EGS.

Thought Break Four

More than 45 years ago, I asked a C-Level executive of a major oil company about what kind of business he was in. He replied that basically he was in the gasoline business. When I pointed out that he would do his customers far better service if he would see his company in the energy business, he argued that I was too revolutionary. No, I replied I am evolutionary, as he should also be. The idea here is that one should forever expand one's horizon, see things in a new light, and seek evolutionary consciousness to better understand one's place in the world. Realistically, oil will play a diminished role as a source of energy in the near future, but evolutionary oil companies can play an expanded role as energy providers. Evolutionary vision is critical, as that executive understands today. Think about it.

12: Growing Into the 21st Century

Death of Forecasting Systems

Here we are deep into the 21st Century and action once again has taken the high road over planning. Today, we have action models, action diagrams, action frames, action tools, action strategies, action this and action that, and so forth. After all, what good are plans when it is action that counts. Right? Today, Strategic Action has replaced Strategic Planning as a domain of the emerging evolutionary model of Executive Leadership. Therefore, a number of postmodern leaders now regard management as an evolutionary approach dedicated to the search for competitive uniqueness rather than sustainable competitive advantage.

Some leaders now understand that business leadership fails whenever it depends on the best practices of others to attain commercial predictability. Some executives clearly see that the mere copying of derivative models ensures perpetual followership. In business, followership is so dominant that even the leaders succumb to it whenever they adopt the finite programs of losers such as re-engineering, quality, and reactionary cost cutting. After all, thoughtful business analysis reveals that most of these programs arose from troubled companies, not successful ones.

Although these practices offer the promise of certainty, business fads entrap many an unsuspecting executive. Unfortunately, the desire for certainty leads executives to search the past to determine the future. Forecasting results from such concerns. However, in the dynamic evolutionary world that demands Cyber Security, forecasting has become meaningless. In the modern world of speed-of-light fast, electronically-enabled business processes, executives cannot extrapolate the future from the past. Cyber Terro gets in the way. Indeed, hyper-competition has changed all the rules. For example, the start-up company of today can overtake an established leader in a few years. Through Virtual Commerce protected by Cyber Security, every day becomes Captain Kirk's undiscovered territory.

As Richard David Hames (1994) reasoned, Appreciative Systems forgo forecasting for scenario setting. But scenario setting requires an organization ecologist to carefully examine certain predetermined consequences by identifying and comprehending underlying phenomena. As mentioned earlier, this person becomes the EIO. Scenario setting must replace forecasting because Information Technology has made change unpredictable in business and life in general.

Through forecasting, management uses quantitative information about the past as a basis for understanding the future. Forecasting focuses on qualitative certainties, disguises uncertainties, and often conceals risks. Forecasting fosters inertia by moving from simplicity to complexity and deriving the qualitative from the quantitative. But the past is not the future. To think otherwise is a formula for failure. Unfortunately, this is exactly what managers do whenever they revert to forecasting to determine their market opportunities for product development and manufacturing. They commit the first mistake of business planning by extrapolating the past into the future.

On the other hand, scenario setting focuses on uncertainties while acknowledging their impact. Scenario setting clarifies risks, encourages flexibility and responsiveness, and moves from complexity to simplicity and the qualitative to quantitative. For executives, scenario setting results in logical pictures of the future rather than guesses based on past history.

Rise of Electronic Registration

As we have previously seen, Electronic Commerce offers the hope of hyper-growth through the adoption of Virtual Commerce, business operations 24 hours a day, seven days a week. Unfortunately, Virtual Commerce endangers the unprepared organization. As e-commerce reduces the dependency on paper-based work flows in favor of electronic documents and transactions, intellectual property, critical business information, and personal documents become increasingly exposed to damage, loss, fraud, unauthorized alteration and duplication, and the loss of audit trails. It is fair to say that E-Commerce escalates Cyber Security challenges.

Many of business and personal documents require electronic registration to baseline their integrity. Using special encryption keys and algorithms, companies such as Peter Robinson's and Ray Newkirk's ElectroNote provide third party authentication services that certify the integrity of electronic documents and transactions. Intellectual property, electronic promotions, invoices, sales programs, insurance documents, letters of credit, contracts, government fillings, insurance documents, electronic mail, trading partner and service level agreements, credentialing and verification, loan processing, employment applications, key escrow, and sensitive record archiving represent the types of electronic documents requiring such registration. Companies like ElectroNote sell electronic notary and digital authentication services to businesses engaged in EC and individuals using personal computers on networks. Cyber Security is central to the success of such initiatives.

Several trends indicate the increasing requirement for Electronic Registration as a component of the postmodern business model. The global spread of Electronic Commerce in government and industry has increased the need to certify special business documents and transactions as a range of documents are increasingly altered, stolen, and contested. Moreover, as an increasing number of companies employ Electronic Commerce, they integrate electronic transactions and imaging in their business processes. This increases the need for extensive Cyber Security interventions to protect the electronic audit and registration services necessary to support business continuity programs.

Moreover, the ever-increasing number of Personal Computers in homes attached to networks, now numbering over 200+ million in the United States alone, raises the need for special Cyber Security based electronic registration services to protect individuals from unscrupulous hackers, criminals, and identity thieves. Obviously, records are altered daily by accident or deliberately by those who desire to corrupt confidential information to gain something or just for the fun of it.

The increasing need to notarize and authenticate intellectual property, business transactions, confidential files and records, and personal documents point to the emerging need to electronically register and authenticate documents of origin. Additionally, the government has passed legislation calling for the creation of an encryption key escrow industry to protect electronic information from fraud, loss, and theft.

Information Technology offers speed; but with speed comes error. The speed of E-Commerce changes the way businesses operate. Executives and managers make decisions quicker; businesses enter into contracts quicker; customers order products faster; vendors make proposals more rapidly; business transactions flow more freely, and disagreements, price deductions, fraud, and law suits increase just as rapidly. Moreover, with the increasingly open environment enabled by E-Commerce technologies, the expanding free flow of ideas characterizes the global community of Virtual Commerce. Therefore, everyone must move more quickly to register their intellectual property and thus protect their rights as businesses or individuals. We really have not been here before. What we do know, however, is that we need more extensive and robust Cyber Security than ever before.

13: Systems Management as an EGS

Bela Banathy (1989) reasoned that Evolutionary Guidance exists "as a dynamic process of giving direction to the evolution of human systems" (p. 291). C-Level executives engage in evolutionary guidance whenever they dynamically give direction to the evolution of their organizations. Through evolutionary guidance, executives develop in Human Activity Systems, i.e., organizations, various capacities and capabilities which recreate and empower social systems (meaning corporations) as Evolutionary Guidance Systems (EGS). These systems consist of at least nine dimensions:

(1) social action;
(2) economic;
(3) moral;
(4) wellness;
(5) educational;
(6) scientific;
(7) technological;
(8) aesthetic, and
(9) political.

Evolutionary Guidance leads to a global human recreation in that it develops the capacity and human capabilities to:

1. Nurture the multi-dimensional development and actualization of individuals and societal systems;
2. Extend the boundaries of human cooperation and compromise in respect to freedom, justice, economic and social well-being, and political participation;

1. increase societal systems cooperation, integration and conflict resolution through non-violence while respecting the "diversity of our cultures and societal systems";
2. Engage in the "design of societal systems that can build the

kind of systemic capacity and human capability described here" (p. 292).

Strategically, the Evolutionary Guidance Systems (EGS) Model of organization human systems offers executives a powerful framework for guiding their enterprises well into the 21st Century and beyond. Reflecting on his notion of evolutionary guidance, Banathy asks a couple of "What if?" questions. For example:

1. "What would happen if the idea of Evolutionary Guidance Systems became reality?"
2. "What would happen if the SMI HAS would engage in purposeful evolution in all the nine dimensions proposed previously?" (p. 292).
3. How would such systems impact the development of Cyber Security?

The following section describes the organizing vision of the Systems Management Institute (SMI) as the impetus to become the idea evolutionary guidance system (EGS). Although we do not directly answer Banathy's questions, it describes the design of the SMI Evolutionary Guidance System, the dimensions comprising that EGS, and the executive process of designing the EGS. Eventually, I will describe what happened to SMI as a HAS engaging in purpose seeking evolution. Thus far we are satisfied with the experience of founding and guiding the company, moving from Information Technology and Management Consulting to Systems Management coaching and development. While more recognized companies have dimmed the lights, SMI has succeeded in very turbulent times.

SMI as an EGS

The Charter of SMI identifies our organizing values as a business enterprise. Indeed, our values inform the formation of our Charter. We formulated the Charter within the Human Systems perspective which focuses on expansionism and evolution rather than reductionism. As a Human Statement, the Charter advances an attitude that values each person as a unique being in the foundation of society. We value people as persons of uniqueness rather than as reproducible objects or subjects of other agencies such as the state, the government, the corporation, the church, or the military. The guiding notion informing the SMI Charter: People are more important than ideas. For SMI, this is the ultimate idea. It is the organizing ideal.

As the Founder, I did not charter SMI as a religion rigid ideology. While a significant number of psychologists, sociologists, theologians, and yes, everyday gurus, speak about self-realization, they frequently mean it in the reductive sense as when an initiate belongs to a particular school of thought or maintains a specific affiliation to a localized community even expanding on a global scale.

Within SMI, self-actualization refers to the continuous self-guided evolution of the person participating in a process of purpose seeking, self-directed, evolutionary unfolding unique to the person but shared via process with the entire human family. Unlike other enterprises, SMI holds that business remains above all else a particularly human affair, and is both participatory and purposeful.

SMI evolved out of my vision and hope for a better world characterized by an improved quality of life. I viewed the traditional corporate vocation as both too constrained to benefit from the vast stores of human potential already available within most companies and too open to the annihilation of self-actualization through the spiralic reductionism of accepted management thinking.

I experienced the corporate world as an ideology through which particular human systems strive to maintain asymmetrical relations of power even in opposition to the stated values of the enterprise. In this often chaotic world, I found that management often sacrificed individuality for illusory consensus disguised as cooperation and team building. I came to see that the common unspoken goals fueling

Leadership at the pinnacle of decision making had become archaic and self-defeating. The quest for personal aggrandizement through the attainment of wealth of historical portions, often bordering on the excessively pathological, and the proliferation of a personal power that reduces the intrinsic value of the lives of employees ultimately became the characteristic summit of human achievement.

SMI abandoned the direction of this too frequently traveled path to human weakness, pain, and emptiness. Rather, we chose a new path for expressing and fulfilling our human potential to be and do more, and to lay the things of a child aside as St. Paul urged. To this end, I designed a new enterprise model that promotes the welfare of those persons associated with the company, including staff, clients, and anyone crossing our path. SMI evolved from the attempt to design this model.

In the beginning, I chartered SMI out of the desire to work for the betterment or self-evolution of human society by extending the General Systems vision into the business environment, whether corporate, academic, religious, or political. For us, the Human Systems vision offers an expansionist vision of human betterment (Boulding, 1985) in all sectors of human enterprise.

SMI cuts across contrived boundaries by refusing to restrict itself to only one area of enterprise such as business or education. Advocating a truly systemic vision, we had to apply our principles to all domains of enterprise, regardless of the narrowly defined goals of any domain. As this system's philosophy evolved to inform the collective vision of the Institute, many members embraced it. As the character of the Institute began to emerge from this vision, we adopted a Charter.

Early Difficulties

The milestone that marked the apparent consensus over the early Charter also marked the official birth of SMI. The early members of SMI clearly understood what they opposed in the corporate world and what they wished that world to become. They were not ambiguous about their feelings. In this sense, SMI became the vehicle carrying us all to a better and more fulfilling professional life in a competitively profit driven world.

It soon became apparent to many in the Institute, however, that consensus really meant compromise and cooperation really meant follower-ship in the worst sense of the word. Consensus did not exist, other than in the imagination of everyone. As people changed their views and attitudes for whatever reason, more openly expressed themselves, or changed their minds about statements in the Charter, the consensus of one day became the painful conflict of the next. Today's solution was indeed tomorrow's problem. Awareness about the emptiness of traditional corporate life did not mean enough to inject a dose of reality into the SMI vision. To launch a new enterprise, the members needed something more than childlike murmurings about corporate life, something more substantial than merely recognizing that something may be terribly wrong with one's own professional life.

In becoming authentic, the SMI Charter required more than an apparently visionary, idealized statement about the existence of the Institute. Ultimately, our first Charter remained an insufficient model that begged the call for action. It was the complaint informed document of some over aged kids. Throughout this awareness stage, SMI suffered through a painful period of revolving door trauma as many persons entered and departed the young company.

Even with its Charter, the Institute still failed to offer a practical program to benefit all members. Inspired by its Charter, many members sharing a similar nontraditional corporate awareness affiliated with the Institute. However, as the number of applicants far outstripped the client base required to support them, SMI had to pull back and again re-examine itself and its Charter. Although we had become a welcome watering hole for many coming in from the corporate wilderness, we had not yet become a viable business enterprise.

Through this stage of reflective self-examination and ever-increasing self-awareness, SMI as an idealized Human Activity System began to understand that its members had to do more than become aware of the Institute's values and their role in clarifying these. For the Institute to succeed, its members had to attain the requisite depth or maturity. The members had to walk the talk consistently to be ready to realize the chartered values of the Institute as enduring operational principles. I finally saw it: All members had to see the Charter as a call to action rather than as an organizing slogan.

Since this leap from conceptualization to action appeared immense, many failed to make it. They remained content to follow the lead of others and minimize their individual contributions to the success of SMI as an environment of evolutionary unfolding. Still others insisted on being leaders. They failed to cross the consciousness-awareness gap. They failed to understand that if one "must" be a leader, one should not be a leader. It is the situation that promotes leadership, not ambition. Banathy's (1989) distinction rung true in our own corporate experience:

> Understanding relatedness and interdependence in the global context is global awareness. Having the intent, the will, the capacity, and the capability to relate to all and integrate with all else in the global system of humanity is the hallmark of global consciousness. Developing individual and collective global consciousness is the common task of individuals, the various societal systems, and the whole of human community (p. 290).

Although many SMI members understood the concept of "relatedness and interdependence in the global context" as a result of unfulfilling corporate careers, some lacked the intent, the will, the capacity, and the capability to relate to all and integrate with all else in the global SMI system of humanity, a subset of the global system of humanity. Accordingly, we expanded the Charter to encourage personal maturity and action leading to the attainment of global consciousness, something more profound than self-realization. As the Founder, I now understood that global consciousness is the defining characteristic of a global corporation.

The Charter had to guide a self-directed evolutionary process that moved people from mere awareness to deep consciousness through living transformation. As expected, this purpose seeking evolutionary process challenged everyone significantly. Closing the gap between awareness and consciousness so that SMI members could authentically embark on the path to global-consciousness and attain a richer quality of life was difficult. It meant that everyone had to ignite themselves using their own self-directed evolutionary consciousness. This deeply challenged the personal, self-systems psychology of each person. In the words of my friend Gene Kerfoot, each person has to engage a process of re-decision.

Evolutionary consciousness addressed only one aspect of the wider evolutionary domain that SMI now desired to signify by its character. Each aspect required our serious attention if we expected the evolutionary process to take hold and become fruitful. Once again, I remembered Bela Banathy with the wonderful Saybrook Graduate School. Professor Banathy (1989) identified the three principal components of the evolutionary domain as:

(1) evolutionary vision and guiding images;

(2) evolutionary competence, and

(3) evolutionary guidance systems.

While evolutionary consciousness leads us to see that we equally share responsibility for our own unique survival through mutual interdependence, evolutionary competence requires a commitment to systems education. We do not become competent by accident. Evolutionary competence builds from commitment. Informed through evolutionary competence, evolutionary vision and guiding images flow freely from evolutionary consciousness. In this regard, the EGS acts as the enabler system that empowers the purpose seeking evolution of Human Activity Systems towards human betterment for all. From its inception SMI desired to be an EGS that seeks the betterment of all.

The evolutionary perspective elaborated the dynamics characterizing Human Activity Systems in which each of the four components outlined above engage each other and thus become interdependent:

(1) evolutionary consciousness;
(2) evolutionary vision;
(3) evolutionary competence, and
(4) evolutionary guidance systems.

Imbalances within the interaction of the components suggest opportunities for purpose seeking evolution if addressed. Or if ignored, they suggest constraints on evolutionary consciousness and human betterment. If we fail to connect evolutionary awareness with consciousness, our Human Activity Systems, our organizations, will ignore their evolutionary potential.

Igniting everyone to action via evolutionary consciousness, the Charter required a model to guide the design of SMI as an interactive and interdependent participative Evolutionary Guidance System, a system chartered to guide its components to self-directed evolution and human betterment. Banathy's (1989) EGS model became the light in the darkness.

Subsequently, through the cooperation of all members we achieved some "agreement," something very fuzzy in Human Activity Systems. We adopted a multi-domain plan to design the EGS of Systems Management Institute. As our overarching goal, we committed to make the idea of Evolutionary Guidance Systems a reality in SMI by design. Additionally, with SMI now seen as an evolutionary Human Activity System, we desired to engage in purpose seeking, self-evolution in all the nine dimensions identified in Banathy's (1989) model.

Cooperative Commitment to Design Inquiry

The realization that consensus offered only a fleeting hope at best startled the early members of the company who formerly believed that consensus meant more than it did. However, we soon realized that the dynamics of human change would lead SMI to flexibility and growth. Moreover, we quickly perceived that conflict, change, and disagreement offered a foundation for success if we employed design inquiry to introduce purpose seeking guidance at the most critical times.

In retrospect, the stormy inception of SMI became invaluable in teaching us several formative lessons. While many corporations established strategic initiatives based on profit, SMI established such initiatives based on an openly discussed value system that exceeded, but respected, the profit motive. As a business enterprise, we regarded profit as a crucial but not the sole motive for urging any of our members to succeed. Contrary to common principles of ultimate capitalism, profit still had not become the driving principle of the Institute. Although important, and a vital management metric, more intangible factors influenced corporate formation and continuous evolution.

Behind the cloud of obscurity, SMI rested upon a platform of embedded values cutting across several cultures, personal experiences, and corporate ideals. Agency Theory was in play; people do join organizations for a wide range of conflicting values. Among the frequently conflicting values, SMI members agreed that a reciprocal relationship had to exist in which the executives supported the goals of the offices comprising the Institute and the offices in turn supported goals of the C-Level executives. They were, after all, interdependent. Both the SMI suprasystem and its components existed in an interdependent relationship that encapsulated the workplace relationships of each person in the Institute. Our managers soon realized that the higher they ascended the management ladder, the greater became the number of persons they had to serve.

Our Charter expressed the ideal that managers worked for their people. Management success required employee success. Following from this Principle of Co-Success people realized that to become successful they had to share success, SMI had to share success with its members and customers to realize its own success. This Principle enables managers to report upward, downward, and vertically in the Institute. As the Founder, I had to minimize the comfortable tendency toward forming closed systems. Understanding this, I worked continually to eliminate dinosaur brain values, attitudes, and thinking from the emerging Institute. The founding of the Systems Management Institute was quite the learning experience.

14: Impact of Cultural Diversity

Challenges to the values of evolutionary consciousness came from a few Asian members of our founding team. For them, the prerequisite levels of interaction, individually, and managerial responsibility outlined in our principles of management did not make sense in a business setting. They felt that such ideas belonged solely to the intimate, nuclear family. Moreover, since they tended toward cultural exclusivity and social closure, they had difficulty bridging the concept of social consciousness.

In culturally diverse environments, successful group leaders recognize the powerful influence of ethnicity when attempting to more fully understand the identity of an individual group member. "Ethnicity refers to a common ancestry through which individuals have evolved shared values and customs. It is deeply tied to the family, through which it is transmitted (McGoldrick & Giordano, 1996)." I realized that by assessing ethnicity, I could better unlock the mystery of personal identity that was impacting our progress in forming the company and I could possibly engender a broader and more culturally expansive perspective.

Several reasons made the assessment of ethnicity increasingly important to me at that time.

First, I knew that the cultural variables of the groups forming our teams and the individual differences among our group members impacted our group work.

Second, I realized that significant developmental differences existed between the African Americans, Hispanic & Latino Americans, Asian and Asian Pacific Americans, Native American Indians, and European Americans forming the

company.

Third, I noted that ethnic groups respond very differently to their experience of discomfort, its symptoms, the communications of discomfort, beliefs about its cause, desired or expected relief, and attitudes about helpers (McGoldrick & Giordano, 1996).

Fourth, I also learned that each group reacted differently to the behavior of the others. For example, the Asians tended to mistrust the upbeat, outgoing, and positive affirming style of the founder preferring a more reserved countenance while others preferred even more openness and emotionalism.

Remembering that Giordano & Giordano (1995) found that group leaders respond better to cultural diversity whenever they bridge the differences between multicultural populations, I initiated a program of cultural education to include everyone in the learning process as team members of one team. Although I realized that it was unnecessary to become expert in all facets of ethnicity, following from Giordano & Giordano (1995), I knew that our group leaders would more successfully lead culturally distinct groups whenever they:

- Gauge the importance placed on ethnicity by group members;
- Validate and strengthen their ethnic identity;
- Employ the support system of group members;
- Become culture brokers;
- Overcome culture camouflage, and
- Understand the advantages and disadvantages of being a member of any given ethnic group.

As the leader in residence, group work with culturally diverse teams becomes extraordinarily dynamic, I had to become extremely adaptable. After all, by now I had learned that the leadership approach I had designed to accommodate one culturally distinct team probably would not work for the teams of different cultural backgrounds. Following from the insights of Andres & Andres (1987), I reasoned that I would better understand each of our culturally distinct teams by comparing their views and values with my own. To this end, I began by examining the defining activities, social relations, processes, sociologies, self-systems psychology of the teams and their members in respect to my view of myself.

In defining activity, I saw that I had to understand each team's attitude about who should make decisions. In defining social relations, I needed to appreciate how the various team members related to others with different statuses. I also had to learn something about how they communicated with others. Finally, I had to discern how the members of each team handled their emotions, and defined and allocated roles. In defining the self, I had to understand how the members of the various teams experienced the nature of individualism. I also had to examine how they believed they should form their identity. Following from Andres & Andres (1987) insights about the multicultural setting, I assessed the social customs of the team members, especially the character of the people and core aspects of their family life, class structure, political patterns, religion, folk beliefs, art, and value systems.

Beyond assessing the core aspects of family life, I felt that I could become more effective as a multicultural leader by comparing and contrasting the important cultural factors of each team. Here I examined each team's orientation to human nature. For example, in considering the relation of humanity to nature, I assessed how my understanding of the character of innate human nature varied from the understanding of each group.

I further assessed the issue of time orientation and its significance for each cultural team by examining each team's temporal focus (time sense) of human life. I also examined the activity orientation of each team by questioning the mode of human activity. Finally, again borrowing an assessment approach from Andres & Andres (1987), I explored the social orientation of each team by questioning the distinctive mode of human relationships. Using this assessment approach enabled me to identify several defining distinctions that may have impacted overall team performance.

For example, in working with the Filipino American team as a distinct culture, a unique Asian American minority population, I used this assessment approach to assist my European American team leaders in identifying and understanding the distinctive elements of the Filipino culture which may have negatively impacted the performance of general group work within the company. The following sections discuss a few of these distinctive elements and cultural dynamics.

Filipino Americans as a Culturally Distinct Population

Working with members of the Filipino American culture is quite different from working with a European American team. Group work with Filipino Americans, as a culturally distinct population, raises several overriding issues that may complicate the group work process.

First, Filipino Americans belong to the Asian American community. As such they inherit many of the issues common to Asian Americans in general. Second, as Asian Americans, Filipino Americans are an ethnic minority group. As Uba (1994) remind us, this implies that Filipino Americans are further challenged to overcome the experiences associated with minority group status. Finally, beyond sharing the Asian American ethnic, Filipino Americans enjoy an extremely rich and unique cultural heritage that is distinctly Filipino and quite unlike other Asians. Andres (1981) makes this point:

> Culturally, the population of the Philippines reflects the great variety of external influences which have impinged upon and blended with the original Malay culture: Arabian, Chinese, Indo-Chinese, Hindu-Indonesian, Spanish-Catholic, and American Protestant. However, the cultural matrix of the modern Filipino was already there at the time of the Spanish Conquista in the middle of the 16th century and may well have been there a thousand years before that.

> Cultural Traits have been borrowed somehow, but combined in such a way that the result is distinctly Filipino. The basic temperament, the lifestyle, the outlook that make up the culture of the Filipino today were already there four centuries ago. Thus, we cannot under-evaluate the strength of the traditional features of Filipino behavior and belief. The lineal village, the strong family unit, the kinship relationships extended through marriage and leadership, the authority vested on family heads and elders were all existent even before Western contact (pg. 2).

As one of the most heterogeneous peoples in the world, a people inhabiting more than 7,100 islands, the Filipino becomes a hybrid of many diverse cultures. For example, as a people, Filipinos speak three primary languages and more than 87 very different dialects. The extensive heterogeneity of the Filipino American population reminds us that the Philippines Islands present a land of opposites. Compared to the European American culture, we find that these opposites are inherent in the seven distinct elements that define the Filipino culture:

(1) values;
(2) basic personality;
(3) basic social unit;
(4) politics;
(5) economics,
(6) technology, and
(7) ecology.

When working with the Filipino American as a culturally distinct population, European American managers have a tough time understanding the social behavior of the Filipino American worker. This confusion is all the more noteworthy whenever these managers attempt to analyze such behavior using their own European American motives and values.

For example, Filipino Americans generally prefer a less autonomous and more dependent way of life rather than one modeled after the European American experience in which the individual can assert his or her own individuality. Unlike many European Americans, the Filipino American inherits a concept of self that is identified with the family. Historically, the Filipino belongs to the family (Andres & Andres, 1987). Following from this, the European American manager further discovers that Filipino Americans are influenced by several complex and overarching cultural traits that impact behavior and decision-making:

(1) Personalism and Hiya;
(2) Familism and Sakop,
(3) Paggalang and Utang na Loop,
(4) Popularism and Sciostat.
(5) Biruan and Parinig,
(6) Tagasalo or Mananalo, and
(7) Nagpapasalo.

Personalism & Hiya in Filipino Americans

As a worker trait, Personalism seriously challenges the group process. I responded to this by recognizing that, for the Filipino American, problem-solving is best managed through personal relations rather than through group exposure, group deliberation, debate, and collegial reasoning. Here I recognized that Personalism conflicts with the European American group work values of openness and expression of feelings. I know that especially in the Filipino American experience, little place exists for confrontation, debate, or the public airing of personal correction and criticism.

Filipino Americans are sensitive to many things. In the workplace this is both good and bad. Understanding that Filipino Americans form a very sensitive culture, a wise group leader exercises extreme care when bringing issues into focus. The concept of shame overtly drives much Filipino American behavior. Hiya, or shame, compels Filipino

Americans to withdraw, hold back, and otherwise remain quiet for fear of embarrassment. Contrary to the obvious strengths inherent in many forms of Western oriented group design and strategy, successful group leadership with Filipino Americans requires the confidential, one-on-one, personal touch - even in the group setting. Filipino social systems can be rigidly controlled.

Familism & Sakop in Filipino Americans

Familism also challenges the group process. "Sakop" behavior (in-group behavior) is stressed over individual behavior and individuality in general. Wise group leaders respond by recognizing that Filipino Americans hold the welfare and interest of the family above the welfare and interest of the individual and the community. The Filipino experiences the family as the first line of defense against a dangerous and hostile world. Andres (1985) reminds us in the West that the family is the one place where Filipinos can cover one's faults rather than expose them.

Working with this culturally distinct population, the group leader leads within a framework of beliefs which holds that the family alone is the basis for group action. For the Filipino American, nearly all group activities must center on the family, not on the individual Filipino American. Moreover, it is the family working together and safely supporting each other, not the individual participant, who will resolve important matters. The group leader capitalizes on this strength by building into a powerful group design the precondition that success and failure will be "sakop" oriented.

Paggalang & Utang Na Loop in Filipino Americans

Through the attitude of "paggalang," in a way related to "sakop", Filipino Americans respect the opinions of those who are elders, in authority, or peers. "Paggalang" is so pervasive that Filipino Americans will consistently respect the word of authority over the truth of another not in authority, even if the one in authority is wrong. The European American group leader needs to recognize that the most powerful moral imperative in Filipino American culture is "utang na loob" - the debt of gratitude. For the Filipino American, issues do not matter; it is personal allegiance to the head of the family, or one in authority that matters.

Popularism & Sociostat in Filipino Americans

Popularism, or small-group centeredness, is the fourth significant challenge facing European American group leaders when working with Filipino Americans. For Filipino Americans, popularity is regarded as a high honor. Filipino Americans generally strive for acceptance from their families, close knit friendships, and professional peer groups. This striving for popularity leads to the tendency termed "sociostat" through which the Filipino tends to remain in the same group at the same level of participation, perpetually if possible (Andres, 1885). Since it may become unpopular to stand out above one's peer group, Filipino Americans do not become aggressively competitive and generally remain content to seek "SIR" - smooth interpersonal relationships, and not rock the boat.

Biruan & Parinig in Filipino Americans

While many in the West believe in the rule of law and order, Filipino culture is guided by the sanctions of shame. Ultimately, for the Filipino, objective truth is less important than the dignity of the person. Truth is usually managed through acts of teasing or "biruan" and "parinig," meaning, indirectly speaking the truth. Hence, morality is based on group centeredness or group thinking, not on individual judgment. What is right or wrong is determined by one's in-group, not usually oneself. The conscience is influenced externally from the outside, i.e., the group, rather than through self-reflection since the Filipino American generally experiences a high need to conform to group think and otherwise avoid shame or disgrace.

Tagasalo or Mananalo in Filipino Americans

Since Filipinos believe so strongly that one must fit in, the childhood development process differs from that of children in the West. For example, the imperative to fit in often occurs at the expense of a child's process of individual differentiation within the family. While European American group leaders may value the concepts "degree of differentiation" (French, 1977) and the more technical "undifferentiated ego mass," (Bowen, 1978), Filipino Americans may view these expressions as ethnocentric, negative, or cultural relativistic. Their explicit behavior certainly rejects them.

We learn from Arellano-Carandang (1987) that Filipino Americans prefer a more descriptive metaphor of Filipino personal boundary management like fried eggs versus hard boiled eggs. This metaphor more adequately and positively compares the Filipino view of optimum boundary management, the fried eggs, to the European American view, hard boiled eggs.

Rather than viewing a situation as violating an individual's right of differentiation, Filipino Americans view their situation as one of exaggerated "tagasalo" or "mananalo," referring to the type of person who comes to the rescue or takes care of someone. In this case, an individual reduces his or her differentiation by compulsively and spontaneously seeking approval through achievement.

Nagpapasalo In Filipino Americans

According to Arellano-Carandang (1987), "tagasalo" presents an even greater challenge to the European American. It creates the "nagpapasalo," or the one needing to be cared for or served. In this case, individual efficacy is a challenge of two extremes, the helper and the helped. The one being helped, the "nagpapasalo," encourages the compulsive helper, the "tagasalo," and the compulsive helper further reduces the autonomy of the one being helped. From the European American perspective, both individuals have a problem of undifferentiated ego mass. However, from the Filipino American perspective, the situation may not be so severe.

Positive Leadership Filipino Americans

As we can see from this brief introduction, the Filipino American population is culturally distinct from the European American. This distinctness represents a generalization of many conflicting values, beliefs, and behaviors manifested by the different subcultures which form the Filipino culture. Although this distinctiveness may not hold for third and fourth generation Filipino Americans, it is real for a great number of them nevertheless.

This distinctness greatly challenges the European American group leader. For one thing, the Filipino American, compared to the European American, prefers an environment in which the Filipino does not assert one's own individuality. This preference takes many forms. Social relationships, communications, and professional perspectives reveal the Filipinos reluctance to be open with strangers.

For example, while European Americans tend to be direct when communicating, Filipino Americans tend to be indirect. In this regard, Filipino Americans prefer body language to verbal expression. Unlike European Americans, Filipino Americans are high context communicators. For the Filipino American, the message is in the person and the context, not the code of language. As a context driven communicator, the Filipino American communicates through silence. For them, a pause conveys as much meaning as a statement of fact. Indirectness is much more valued than directness.

Leading a Filipino American group requires the European American to shift gears. Preventing a conflict of values from erupting, European American group leaders minimize the openness, expression of feelings, nurturing of individuality, and directness which are so characteristic of the group work values of European American thought and practice.

European American group leaders succeed with Filipino Americans whenever they shift their focus from the personal, and potentially embarrassing, in-depth issues of personality and performance to more practical and targeted tasks concerns related to work-skills improvement. Leaders will undoubtedly benefit the workplace by focusing on important practical concerns of everyday living rather than in attacking the characterological dimension of Filipino America workers. In this regard, leaders succeed whenever they use a small group focus to form new peer relationships and build safe environments in which Filipino Americans develop heightened self-esteem. Leadership integrity is crucial to success in such an environment.

Unquestionably, success in leading a diverse team requires a measure of adaptability, abundant practical wisdom, and sincere interest in others. Complementing this, the wise leader of diverse teams understands his role as a designer of the future. After all, as "a creative, decision-oriented disciplined inquiry," design offers an intelligent process for bringing diverse cultures together to intelligently design their alternative futures.

Within this environment of complex diversity, the founding teams of SMI agreed that design taken as "a creative, decision-oriented disciplined inquiry" becomes the missing link in the development of the SMI Charter. Banathy (1989) writes:

I suggest that design is the missing inquiry in purposeful societal evolution where the key problems are:

1. How to bring intention and design together;
2. How to transform evolutionary images into functional designs of societal systems; and

1. How to produce structures and societal/ organizational processes and arrangements that, in fact, realize the future that we intend to bring about (p. 294).

Here in this passage, Banathy has touched upon the three key formative problems facing SMI at its inception. These three problems were the same challenges that I had sought to overcome from the beginning. Mulling over Banathy's prophetic words in light speed, I enjoyed one of those wonderful "I see it" moments, you know, those sudden insights that instantly make your world about a thousand pounds lighter. I knew now that I had been working in the dark. There was more to this "design stuff " than meets the eye. As I applied Banathy's insight to my current situation, I found that I now had a clear plan of action for moving SMI forward along the reliability path to success. Through the sage wisdom of Banathy of the Saybrook Graduate School, I could now jumpstart the process, but a lot of work still remained.

Leveraging our agreement on the importance of design in formulating an organizing Charter, the SMI team engaged in an ever evolving design inquiry to design the SMI EGS. Clearly, we all wanted SMI to become a purpose seeking Human Activity System guided by both Banathy's EGS model and Vickers model of appreciative systems. In keeping with the vision of a better company, I now understood that, somehow, we had to bring our intention and design together. We had to design an enterprise-wide Human Activity System that would enable us to evolve the type of company we intended to build.

Doing so, we would transform evolutionary images of future designs of SMI into functional designs with the requisite societal systems and subsystems. Understanding that design never achieves its horizon, (according to Banathy's principle of retreating design horizon, we went to work on building and implementing designs that enabled SMI to function as an adaptable and continually evolving company. As we built the concept of purpose seeking evolution into our functional environment, we gradually found that some designs constrained process evolution while others enriched it. Most interestingly, the constraining designs heightened the challenge of skill overspecialization while the enriching designs heightened the challenge of skill over-generalization.

Creating a model of the executive team as an Evolutionary Guidance System, we found that SMI became more robust and adaptable, and purpose seeking. As a goal, we wanted our EGS to enable SMI members to participate in the evolutionary unfolding of the company, as they participated in their own evolutionary unfolding. This was definitely an exciting concept that ignited the imagination and participation of most executives and employees.

Capitalizing on the insights of Banathy, we began to organize the structures, societal/organizational processes, and arrangements that would carry the company to success, keep it viable, and enable it to evolve. In fact, we had to do all the things necessary to realize the future that I intended to achieve with the participation of executives, employees, customers, and regulators.

Working the three issues so well-articulated in Banathy's vision, the SMI Charter more rapidly became an historic agreement. Shortly after, while we were busy feeling good about ourselves and what we had achieved through the assistance of Professor Banathy's academic insights, we realized that the Charter would undergo numerous bifurcations in the course of its evolutionary unfolding. Since the Charter mirrored our images of the future, it would bifurcate in step with our images.

Everyone agreed, an evolutionary Charter was a great idea. After all, we had already seen so many charters that were frozen in time. We did not want to be tied down by an immovable artifact of the historical past, as some Charters become. Rather we wanted our Charter to be alive, both enriching and invigorating, and mirroring our own evolutionary unfolding. SMI would certainly become a company of motion. There would be little room for boredom to work its tentacles into our company.

Our Charter reminded us that we would be management advocates reaching out to clients: We go where we were needed but not wanted and would leave when we were wanted but not needed.

Our nearly spontaneous agreement to engage in design inquiry implied a renewed commitment to action. Not only would we design an EGS for SMI, but we would also function as one. We would work to transform design into action. This additional commitment to action, to employ the ideals of the EGS in practice, reframed our responsibilities and simplified our ever-expanding agendas. This commitment would also enable us to bring intention and design together, transform evolutionary images into functional designs of SMI's societal systems, and produce the structures and societal/organization processes and arrangements that would realize the future that we intended to produce.

Conducting a design inquiry into SMI as an EGS was not going to be easy. For some of us it would become one of the most difficult undertakings of our lives. Fortunately, by this time we all realized that in conducting an EGS-based design inquiry we would have to satisfy at least three conditions to obtain evolutionary competence. Banathy (1987c) writes:

The use of this force for creating a better future and to give a positive direction to our evolution is dependent on three conditions:

1. developing evolutionary consciousness and evolutionary vision and creating positive guiding images of the future;
2. acquiring evolutionary competence through evolutionary learning; and
3. using our competence by designing evolutionary guidance systems in our human activity systems through which we can realize our positive images for the future (p. 24).

"What a group of demands," a few of the executives protested, "another academic to contend with!" "We might as well go to the moon and enter the cheese business." People complained out loud about finding the time to meet the three stark demands of Banathy? They questioned who in the company had the time to acquire evolutionary competence when everyone was busy earning their way through business. They wondered how they were going to find the time to commence evolutionary learning. Others protested: "Are we building a company or are we earning Ph.Ds. in systems thinking?" Complain, complain, complain. All problems, no solutions! What a group, I thought! I need a team, not a mob of complainers.

Not deterred and refusing to back down, I pushed ahead by presenting a plan to free everyone's fingers from the tight grip of the unknown terror that was consuming them. Unknown to them, I realized that in commencing the SMI/EGS design inquiry, we would acquire evolutionary competence through evolutionary learning by combining maintenance learning with adaptability learning,- the evolutionary learning of Banathy (1987c).

In designing our EGS, our management team attempted to actualize the insight of Banathy (1987c). We embarked on a program to nurture evolutionary values and obtain competence in cooperative group interaction, system thinking and action, anticipatory thinking, problem management and system design. Facilitating this program, I formed a design HAS to build an SMI-EGS model of the future and conduct the design inquiry. Operationally, I wanted the management team to become the EGS of SMI.

Thought Break Five

Lately I have become perplexed by the current management idea that diversity is great because it means improved profitability. "So let's be diverse," as one executive told me, "we will capture the global market share." It seems that management has overlooked the added cost of bringing a diverse workforce together to accomplish its objectives. Let me explain.

Although it has only nine letters, diversity is such a big word. Diversity can be seen from many perspectives, and in management it is often seen from only one of them. Whatever it means to advocates in corporate America, it does not mean togetherness, unity, universality, uniformity, similarity, homogeneousness, conformity, consensus, coming together, or anything else that most people think whenever they talk about making many diverse individuals come together to carry out a singular organizing vision.

More precisely, diversity is all about ensuring the multiform, the dissimilar, the divergent, and separate. True to its nature in organizations, diversity is about maintaining the boundaries between different kinds, forms, or characters. Thus, the noble adherence to diversity is counter-intuitively about establishing those processes, policies, mechanisms, procedures, and opinions that separate one person from the other in difference to the person's inherent divergent characters. Rationally, diversity is not about establishing corporate programs at the superficial level of experience that seek to minimize the diverse nature of individuals while simultaneously capitalizing on such uniqueness.

Think about your own organization's experience with Diversity. Does it employ programs that seek to put everyone on an even playing field by minimizing the authentic divisive nature of cultural difference? Or does your organization employ diversity programs that really seek to understand and master the stark reality of human differences in communications styles, defining values, management styles, and a host of other characteristics?

If you think long and hard about it, you will find that a lot of corporate diversity programs are masked efforts to maintain asymmetrical relations of power on behalf of the executive team and at the expense of a certain established groups within the organization. Is this not the main function of most Human Resources Management groups?

I have plenty of misgivings about such references to Diversity, not without reason. In reality, not everyone can get alone with someone who expresses an extremely different view of life. It can be very threatening, and for good reason whenever core cultural factors come into play. Balancing Diversity requires considerable knowledge and great skill. Think about the experience required to manage a team of workers from India, Italy, Israel, England, France, Peru, Philippines, Hungary, Russia, Poland, Mexico, Egypt, Kenya, and the United States. How does a leader mold such multi-cultural diversity into a cutting-edge competitive team that wins in the marketplace? Diversity programs counter-intuitively are anything but Diversity programs in that they attempt to reduce diversity. Diversity management is difficult. Think about it.

15: Conclusion to Part 1

In Part One, I discussed the brave new world of Cyber Security and explored the hyper-growth formula suggested by the disruption of Virtual Commerce. I argued that executive success requires a more relevant model of executive leadership for the 21st Century, the postmodern business era. I further argued that executives should view their senior team as an Appreciative Evolutionary Guidance Systems. The EGS model advances scenario setting over forecasting and establishes the Enterprise Intelligence Officer as the organization ecologist who replaces the Director of Management Information Services to become a core business executive. As a case study, future chapters will discuss how the concepts in Part One empowered a single company, the Systems Management Institute.

16: Part Two: Appreciative EGS

Part Two examines how the founders of a successful consulting company employed an Appreciative Evolutionary Guidance Systems approach to design their firm. Part Two further describe how senior executives linked systems thinking with systems practice, thought with action, and Cyber Security, to balance the core dimensions of corporate life in accomplishing both business and personal evolutionary goals.

Beyond this, Part Two examines the challenges involved in forming and exercising such an inspired model of business life. Here I discuss the pitfalls and tarpits encountered along the way as I endeavored to build an invigorating work atmosphere, one that consistently mobilized innovation and change, motivated staff to manage themselves and their tasks well, freed managers to manage others well, and encouraged everyone to communicate very effectively every day. Here I lay the groundwork for designing a unified Continuous Performance Management and Insider Threat Prevention Cyber Security Model as the core of the technological dimension.

In Part Two, Chapters Twelve, Thirteen, Fourteen, Fifteen and Sixteen discuss the SMI charter, the impact of cultural diversity on the appreciative systems model, the hidden nature of human performance and its impact on a new enterprise, the SMI enhanced meaning of competence, and the bases of competence informing the SMI vision.

17: Counterintuitive Nature of Performance

As we jumped into our challenge with all reckless abandon, I soon discovered that the three domains of professional expertise, competence, proficiency, and performance, impacted our efforts to design the Evolutionary Guidance System of SMI. Out of the three domains, performance remained the least argumentative. While everyone on the project continually debated the meaning of competence and proficiency, the same people believed they could easily distinguish acceptable from unacceptable performance.

Performance pretty much spoke for itself. Although we used several measures of performance, the proverbial business bottom-line made this much abundantly clear to all of us in management. Performance as a measure of success was even more salient than productivity, to which it was often conversely proportional. Interestingly, we found that in some situations while productivity increased, performance would decrease. One did not necessarily equate with the other.

As the program to design our own EGS unfolded, I came to see that the Problem of Performance impacted all our activity, as it impacts all human activity. Although performance was intimately linked to team and individual competence at SMI, it had gone beyond this to become the standard or criteria of our individual and organization success. For us, performance had become the pervasive challenge that defined the difference between success or failure and even between competitive leverage and strategic weakness. I had always believed that everyone in management well understood the meaning of performance. Back

then I assumed that performance was one of those self-evident truths that required little clarification. Even children clearly understood its ramifications, I argued.

Commentators have written books about it. Specialists have conducted numbing research on it. At one time or another, we all have run up against problems with performance and have been found wanting. Either our performance was insufficient, found lacking, was under expectations, or occasionally disappointed someone. Indeed, if your performance has never been found wanting, you have gained little opportunity for development. Think about it.

The Problem of Performance

Newkirk's Law 137: Performance Paradox: While great performance lays the foundation for failure, inadequate performance paves the road to great performance.

Most of my thinking about performance was pretty much fixed until that day Peter Robinson asked me: "What is Performance, and what do you mean, Ray, by the Problem of Performance?" Until that day, I just assumed that it was an intuitive term that no one debated. Wrong again. I should have known better by then. Great, I thought, I must be on the road to great performance if I fell short here because my current level of Performance was certainly inadequate.

Webster's tells us that the word performance refers to "the manner in which or the efficiency with which something reacts or fulfills its intended purpose," or "the execution or accomplishment of work, acts, feats." Webster's further relates performance to competence. In this respect, then, the Problem of Performance refers to the problem of execution of work, and one's competence in executing work.

For obvious reasons Webster's answers to Peter's questions did not reveal enough to enable either one of us to do much about resolving the Problem of Performance at SMI. When we thought more deeply about Peter's questions, we came up against the challenges of execution, accomplishment, competence, and a host of related issues that led to even more difficult questions. Being mere common definitions, Webster's answers got us nowhere closer to where we needed to be to more adequately understand our immediate Problem of Performance.

Historically, efforts to answer the many questions associated with the problem of human performance in organizations have uncovered a view of performance in which efficiency is seen as a short run criterion of effectiveness. One cannot be efficient if one is not effective. Here, management experts characterize performance using several attributes of quality, foremost of which are effectiveness and efficiency.

Effectiveness by far is the core attribute of great leadership and management success. If we are to understand this relationship, then, we must go even deeper and ask about the dynamics that form this relationship between effectiveness and efficiency, meaning, the relationship between doing the right thing, effectiveness, and doing things right, efficiency. Indeed, what are the dynamics that make performance acceptable? Finding answers to Peter's questions meant that we had to go underneath the mere criteria and examine the dynamics of the entire problem situation. This, my friend, is a systems design challenge!

The Problem of Performance Explored

The Problem of Performance impacts all human activity. At the beginning of the 21st Century, this problem still challenges academics, behavioral scientists, organization theorists, and researchers in the management sciences. In the consulting specialty of Organization Effectiveness, performance remains a broad concept. It touches leadership, conflict, motivation, expectations, perceptions, enrichment, outcome criteria, rewards, goal attainment, individual growth and development, and a host of other related concepts. Interestingly, Webster's Dictionary links performance with competence. Even philosophers and theologians continually explore the issue of human performance. Clearly, the Problem of Performance remains a universal and timeless struggle.

Nowhere is this problem more apparent than in leadership and management. In these arenas, the Problem of Performance has become intimately linked to the challenge of team and individual competence. Here performance has become the standard or criteria of individual and organization success. Within the triumvirate of (1) management thinking, (2) team execution, and (3) individual action, performance is the pervasive challenge that defines the difference between success and failure and even between competitive leverage and strategic weakness.

For entrepreneurs, attempts at solving the Problem of Performance frequently stir the stew of management complexity. Rather than advancing a solution, these attempts merely succeed in producing a large mix of challenging questions for which answers seem obvious and intuitive on the surface but underneath turn out to be everything else. For example, how do you respond to the question: What is performance? And where does performance come from? What are its defining characteristics? What is its relationship to leadership, behavior, and goals? Does performance mean the same for groups as it does for individuals? Does it mean the same for organizations as it does groups, or individuals? Better still, does performance mean competence or proficiency? Does it mean effectiveness or efficiency? What are the effects of performance and what are the indicators? Finally, does performance involve particular identifying dynamics?

Searching for answers to any of these questions inexhaustibly uncovers an ever-widening expanse of new questions. However, is this not to be expected of a reality so vital to the success of contemporary 21st Century leadership and management, whether in government, industry or education? At the core of these questions is the single defining issue for leaders: How do we bolster performance in individuals, teams, and organizations, and how do we improve it consistently? This, then, is the substantive echo at the heart of the Problem of Performance. The improvement of performance is the reoccurring leadership imperative and often its most singular nightmare. Realistically, we can ascribe all failings in leadership and management practice to failings in performance, at the individual, group, or organization levels.

Over the years conceptual innovators concerned with the Problem of Performance have aggressively attacked these questions offering answers in the language of performance management, performance measurement, organization behavior, organization development, leadership, and competence. Their efforts have illuminated the Problem of Performance by delivering theories and models to assist managers and their teams with improving performance in organizations.

Eventually, these efforts formed a description of performance as the: "desired result of behavior." In this view, performance becomes the efficiency with which we fulfill the intended purpose, where efficiency is seen as the ability to produce outputs with minimum use of inputs and is expressed as ratios such as cost-time, cost-output, and benefit-cost. Efficiency then becomes a short run criterion of effectiveness. Thus, a team must be efficient to be effective.

Fundamentally, performance is characterized using several attributes of quality. Foremost among these are effectiveness and efficiency. While efficiency has received the majority of management attention over the last several decades through the introduction of numerous organization change and re-engineering approaches, effectiveness by far is the core attribute of great leadership and management success. Many of us know by now that efficiency means doing things right and effectiveness means doing the right things. In this sense, then, effectiveness becomes the optimal relationship among production, efficiency, satisfaction, adaptation, and development. Like its sister efficiency, effectiveness also occurs at the individual, group, and organization levels.

While individual effectiveness is task specific, group effectiveness occurs through the sum of the contributions of all its members. Counter-intuitively, organization effectiveness occurs as more than the sum of individual and group effectiveness. Even more interesting, enabled by special systems-inherent synergistic effects, organizations share the potential to achieve even higher levels of performance than that possible through the actions of the sum of their parts.

Management more easily identifies the causes of individual, group, and organization effectiveness when making the distinction between the causes and the indicators of effectiveness.

Optimal balance is the most desirable relationship among the criteria of effectiveness. Moreover, Management wants to achieve optimal rather than maximal balance in any case of more than one criterion. Here we see the causes of individual effectiveness as ability, skill, knowledge, attitude, motivation, and stress and the causes of group effectiveness as cohesiveness, leadership, structure, status, roles, and norms. Furthermore, we see the causes of organization effectiveness as environment, technology, strategic choices, structure, processes, and culture. Informed through Agency Theory and armed with political acumen, management achieves effectiveness by:

- Achieving goals
- Maintaining the core systems processes of input, transformation, output, feedback and adjustment, and environmental adaptation, and
- Responding to the importance of the difference in interests flowing from the diversity of values inherent in the various groups and individuals in the organization.

Dynamics of Performance

Going beyond the definitions of Webster, we discover that factors other than the ability to execute work or the intention to fulfill a purpose influence (a) how we seek or avoid challenges and (b) when we use or develop our skills effectively. We further discover that competence is not a fixed ability. Rather, competence is a dynamic factor of performance that involves a generative capability in which we organize and effectively direct cognitive (intellectual), social, and behavioral skills under many different circumstances. This is especially the case whenever many of these circumstances are stressful, confusing, and unpredictable. Where performance is concerned, a capability is only as good as its execution.

Ancient Success Formula

At the beginning of the 21st Century, management life is nurtured by an ancient formula of business success: Knowledge enabled by tools equals performance. Performance is everything. It is king. It separates the weak from the strong, the prepared from the clueless, the enabled from the powerless, the mindful from the mindless, the victorious from the vanquished, and the successful from the redundant. In today's business life, with most things filtered through the lens of cost versus profit ratios, one's level of performance is the difference between enjoying the fruits of a promising career or suffering the pains of an undesirable job, and the difference between being an inspiring and noble leader or a perennial follower.

This ancient formula is misleading as it blinds many to the tremendous gulf separating knowledge from performance. In current management practice, the ancient formula of business success has become common law, hardly questioned. All of this even though the ancient formula discounts the role of competence in the unfolding of every human life, and all of this even though competence remains the central attribute in the realization of performance.

Still the world suffers through this confusion even though many leaders understand intuitively that without the requisite level of competence, knowledge, even enabled by the best of all possible tools, in itself does not deliver great performance. Your personal history probably attests to this. The media discusses a number of knowledgeable people performing incompetently. After all, incompetence does not necessarily infer stupidity.

Beyond apparent experience, an individual may indeed be very knowledgeable but may, nevertheless, remain too incompetent to perform a task or fill a role well. Competence goes beyond tools and knowledge.

Leadership seeks to improve performance by engaging in several approaches to employee development, some of them quite revolutionary. Training, educating, coaching, mentoring, and consulting represent common approaches to development designed to improve the performance of executives, managers, and the rank and file. More specifically, people take one of two paths to improve performance. Either they attempt to develop the specific personal attributes associated with performance such as credibility, confidence, patience, or execution. Or they attempt to improve the key processes resulting in ever higher levels of performance such as specialized quality assurance and management processes. Occasionally, following a common framework of performance, leaders attempt to follow both paths concurrently.

Reducing these paths to a common framework, however, leaders arrive at the knowledge and tools driven approaches inferred in the ancient success formula. Here, once again, we encounter the two dominant approaches thought to improve performance through the mastery of the specific prerequisites of Leadership, so the common knowledge argues. By the late 20th Century, the performance improvement industry had become an entrepreneurial enterprise conceived in management thinking to directly increase the generation of profits, and indirectly the quality of life through the improved application of tools and techniques.

Today, the leadership and development industry surpasses billions of dollars in annual revenues. Since money talks and B.S. walks, this very substantial industry casts a wide net of influence over leaders in industry, government, and education. In this age of spreading global consumerism characterized by the demand to continually increase profits, everyone rushes to improve performance, and do it quickly, inexpensively and conveniently.

More on the Counterintuitive Nature of Performance

In mastering the dynamics of performance, one of the challenges facing us is the concept of performance itself. Being fundamentally a concept of goal orientation, performance becomes a counterintuitive concept. This counterintuitive nature becomes all the more obvious whenever management makes performance the goal of leadership and focuses on worker ability as the road to performance improvement. Rather than delivering improved performance, the management focus on ability merely calls each person's ability into question. In the end, management counter-intuitively increases the risk of failure by weakening or undermining the worker's confidence in his or her own ability to perform expertly.

In a strange sort of way, the scientific evidence regarding performance is counterintuitive. The reality of the challenge is such that the attainment of the goals of performance requires each of us to individually bolster our confidence in our own ability to accomplish the goals. Otherwise, we will not choose the necessary tasks nor pursue them effectively. By focusing on performance as a goal, however, management achieves the opposite. Moreover, since past performance does not increase a worker's confidence in his or her own abilities to manage current problems or master future challenges, managers who focus on performance ultimately fail to motivate their employees to capitalize on past achievements.

Role of Perception in Performance

When it comes to improving performance, perception is king, even in perceived competence. Beliefs regarding personal abilities are the most central factor in impacting the dynamics of performance. We know from research in the behavioral sciences that:

- Perceived self-beliefs are related to the belief in one's ability to exercise control over task demands and
- Perceived competence is concerned with one's judgments of personal capabilities.

Self-beliefs regarding one's own capability directly impact motivation, affective arousal, and thought processes. As such self-beliefs at least partly govern our performance attainments. Everything being equal, the worker maintaining the strongest self-beliefs of efficacy does best. Unfortunately, by focusing on ability in attempts to improve employee performance, managers weaken the employee's referential self-beliefs of efficacy by implicitly calling them into doubt.

Rather than focusing on performance per se, managers may build employee performance by recognizing that perceived competence is a function of performance and learning, not knowledge.

Focusing on learning rather than performance, or knowledge, management leverages the relationship of performance to learning to improve employee action and management practice. In this case, management uses learning to better focus employees on performance as a means of utilizing, activating, or increasing an employee's learned ability for overcoming obstacles. The dynamics of performance are so inherent in producing the outcome of performance that several influences are now known to govern performance attainment, the most pressing of which include:

- Affective self-evaluation
- Perceived self-efficacy of goal attainment, and
- Personal goal.

Obviously, solving the Problem of Performance is always difficult. Seasoned managers understand that self-referent thought transforms knowledge and abilities into skilled performance whenever perceived confidence in one's abilities is high and self-beliefs in one's own competence is correspondingly high. Unfortunately, by focusing on performance itself as a goal, however, management calls such self-beliefs in competence into question and risks reducing perceived confidence in worker abilities. Thus, by calling into question an employee's self-beliefs regarding the employee's self-efficacy, the self-beliefs erode and self-efficacy decreases. The cycle of behavior is all counter-intuitive. Informed by the dynamics of performance, wise leaders build organization effectiveness by:

- Achieving learning goals
- Maintaining the core systems processes of input, transformation, output, feedback and adjustment, and environmental adaptation
- Responding to the importance of the difference in interests of each employee as such interests build the perceived self-confidence that flows from the diversity of values setting apart the various groups and individuals in the organization.

Performance is more complex than the concept expressed in the ancient and highly under-conceptualized Success Formula: Knowledge enabled by tools equals performance. Unfortunately, this ancient formula is misleading as it blinds leaders to the tremendous gulf separating knowledge from performance. In examining this formula, you begin to uncover the dynamics of leadership and its impact on employee development, especially self-beliefs.

Knowledge, Information, & Power

Although knowledge offers genuine power, in itself such power may negatively impact peak performance when it is separated from an in-depth and noble vision. Innovative leaders more appropriately adopt the systems perspective to better understand the dynamics of group work and build team performance. This is especially the case whenever such leaders understand the pivotal role of the dynamics of competence in the improvement of team performance. For such leaders, the relationship between knowledge, tools, competence and performance is a vital one. This relationship fuels the archetypical question about success and forms the wider relationship linking competence to performance.

For a significant number of business leaders, the dream of convenient and inexpensive knowledge attainment represents the ultimate quest in the campaign to improve performance through knowledge acquisition. Granted the notable exception of state supported mass educational institutions, discount driven and highly technical training companies, and the all too few innovative learning providers, the dream of an inexpensive and convenient knowledge base designed to improve workplace performance goes unrealized.

Beyond the need for a virtual source of knowledge, leaders require an abundance of timely and accurate information to sustain performance. Lacking such information, performance suffers. Over the years, I have learned that information bias and data filtering greatly contribute to many of the problems threatening organizations and their leaders today. Leaders at the pinnacle of decision-making depend on the information they receive to make the critical decisions necessary to ensure the success of their organizations and the projects that support them. For the harried leader, accurate information has become a luxury all too difficult to obtain. Politics, fear, manipulation, insecurity, error, accident, carelessness, and yes, even dishonesty, represent only a few of the challenges plaguing executives as they seek the information necessary to make the right decisions about their organizations at the right times and for the right reasons. Innovative leaders seek improved performance using the expanded view of systems thinking.

Here the smart innovative leaders elaborate the ancient success formula of knowledge and tools by examining the pivotal role of the dynamics of competence in the improvement of group performance. The relationship between knowledge, tools, competence and performance is a vital one. It fuels the archetypical question about success presenting both challenge and opportunity. This wider relationship linking competence to performance is the ultimate success formula for the 21st Century leader.

Thought Break Six

Over the years, I have encountered a lot of confusion about the idea of bringing a new culture into an enterprise to improve competitive performance. The leadership thinking buried in this core management belief leaves me wondering about the nature of the susceptibility that leaders must have to believe in such trends and fads. I silently ask myself the most obvious of questions: How many more years are these leaders going to let themselves be dominated by such thinking, or should I say feelings?

Trends and fads are never a sound basis for doing the difficult things. One has to go deeper into the matter of cultural change and develop a human systems approach for designing a new Human Activity System. This is what changes human work systems. We may never know all we need to know to manage all the many facets of cultural embeddedness in organizations. But we can design enduring Human Activity Systems in response to the kinds of environmental contingencies that imply the need for purpose seeking human systems across all cultures.

For one thing, every organization already has a culture, for good or bad. One cannot simply install a new culture by offering a few workshops, seminars, or social engineering programs. In these instances, the current culture will merely react in some way to the perceived interference. Realistically, cultures change continually. Like Heraclitus and his river, no leader can ever step into the same culture twice.

Change is all around us. It defines our very nature as human beings.

Adding people to an organization or transferring them out changes culture; imparting new knowledge changes culture. Changes in the structure, environment, or processes of a culture change that culture. The point here is that cultures are forever in flux. We cannot prevent a culture from evolving. We can, however, guide the direction of such inevitable change. This is Evolutionary Leadership, or Leadership by Design. Functioning as an Evolutionary Guidance System (EGS), enterprise leadership guides the evolutionary unfolding of organizations. In precisely this way, leaders guide the evolution from one state of culture to another. This is the best anyone can do. Think about it.

18: Enhanced Meaning of Competence

As we have seen in a previous chapter, Webster's Encyclopedic Unabridged Dictionary of the English Language states that competence is sufficiency, as in a sufficient quantity. It also defines it as adequacy. Webster's further refers to competence as the "possession of the required skill, knowledge, qualification, or capacity."

At SMI, we also believe that competence includes all of these hallmarks of excellence. A competent person is adequate to the task, meets the requirement of sufficiency, and indeed possesses the required skill, knowledge, qualification, or capacity to do the job. In this Digital Age marked by rapid and frequent change, aggressive business competition, spreading globalization, rapid innovation, and the dehumanization brought on through the escalating use of technology in the workplace and home, a competent person is a mindful person. Yesterday's standard of competence is insufficient for today and tomorrow. Mindfulness is essential to enjoying a quality lifestyle in a High-Tech Age.

For SMI, competence consists of three defining characteristics. A competent person:

- possesses the requisite knowledge for a given situation;
- applies this knowledge successfully in changing situations as appropriate, and
- possesses the social skills to successfully apply the knowledge proficiently.

Competence, therefore, consists of three overriding components:

- knowledge,
- adjustable correct activity, and
- social acumen.

A competent person is self-directed, communicates well, readily mobilizes innovation and change, clearly possesses the capability to manage or lead team members as situations warrant, and sufficiently designs and plans the future. A competent person is one who makes a difference by producing real results.

Newkirk's Law 137 is worth reflection:

> Incompetent persons and solid tools produce incompetent persons with mediocre tools.

Understanding this, SMI derived our consulting and learning programs from the experience of successful consulting and management practice. Our Applied Intuitive Solutions™ (AIS™) emerge from a solution generation process that flows from consulting practice to content delivery to solution generation, and from competence enhancement to application and to success.

Rather than beginning with theory and textbooks, we begin with powerful insights gained from the industry changing consulting assignments of the Systems Management Institute to inform our AIS™. Leveraging our evidence-based insights, we developed an intelligent environment to assist end-users with solving problems in rapid real-time by eliminating the "problem-solution gap" characteristic of the usual problem-solving approach. Our AIS™ Platform enables clients to leverage significant global consulting experience to build essential skills and competencies more rapidly. Moreover, our Virtual Learning environment emerged to deliver a solid learning experience grounded in the critical workplace skills as reflected in our unique learning content.

Competence & Performance Relationship

As discussed in an earlier chapter, business life is nurtured by an ancient formula of professional success: Knowledge enabled by tools equals performance. Performance is everything. Lacking it, you quickly become redundant. In competitive life, your performance defines your worth. Moreover, performance determines your position along the success ladder of life. The relationship between knowledge, tools, competence, and performance is vital. It fuels the archetypical question that offers both a challenge and an opportunity.

As we have previously seen, people customarily remain blind to the wide gap between knowledge and performance. So quickly they discount the role of competence in the unfolding of every human life. Nevertheless, competence remains the central attribute in the attainment of performance. Lacking competence, knowledge, even enabled by the best of all possible tools, does not necessarily produce noteworthy performance. History offers many examples of smart people doing badly. Obviously, incompetence does not necessarily mean stupidity. Brilliant people also fail, and they fail badly.

In the world of competitive commerce, knowledge attainment is itself a commercial enterprise intended to directly boost the generation of profits and indirectly the quality of life through the improved application of tools. The knowledge and learning industries surpass billions of dollars in annual

revenues. As a consequence, they cast a wide net of influence among leaders in business and government. In this age of fierce competition, characterized by the unforgiving demand to continually grow profits, everyone works to improve performance, and do it quickly, inexpensively and conveniently.

For a large number of business leaders, the dream of convenient knowledge attainment represents the ultimate quest in the campaign to improve performance. However, with the notable exception of state supported mass educational institutions, discount driven and highly technical training companies, and the all too few innovative learning providers, the dream of an inexpensive and convenient knowledge base for improving human performance goes unrealized. The relationship between knowledge, tools, competence and performance is vital. It fuels the archetypical question that presents both a challenge and an opportunity.

Competence, knowledge, and performance are big words. They are charged with emotion, loaded with meaning, and cut across the boundaries of traditional disciplines such as psychology, law, sociology, education, management, and so forth. SMI digs more deeply into the mystery of success to uncover the golden significance of competency-based Virtual Learning. Seizing both the obvious challenge and hidden opportunity of our archetypical question, we have developed competency based Applied Intuitive Solutions™ that energize more completely the knowledge environment of the modern enterprise. By designing practical and innovative competence focused solutions to improve performance, SMI dedicates itself to filling the gap in the knowledge-performance formula, a gap that leaders increasingly recognize to have strategic importance.

As an evolutionary company, SMI provides programs and services inexpensively and effectively to anyone connected to the Internet. Offering a Virtual Problem-Solving Platform, our AIS™ enable management to justify the cost of competence-building investments.

We have designed a mission critical, rapid real-time, skills development Platform that enables organizations to improve profitability by reducing dependence on in-house coaching, consulting, and Training. Indeed, trade experts expect Internet delivered competency development to reduce coaching, consulting, and training costs by an attractive amount over the next several years, perhaps by more than 50%.

Leveraging the Internet to enhance problem solving competence, SMI designed an innovative competence building format termed Action Learning or simply A-Learning. Dr. Newkirk designed Action Learning to improve the competence of individuals and the performance their organizations. These are the consumers of SMI. Through our proprietary, content rich, action oriented Applied Intuitive Solutions™, we deliver multi-path opportunities for developing personal and team competence at a compelling price when compared with other problem solving and skills development methods.

When AIS™ adoption achieves critical mass as an increasing number of participants implement this universe of Applied Intuitive Solutions™, commentators expect Virtual-Problem Solving to become the preferred approach of problem solving for businesses and individuals everywhere. This is an admirable claim.

While executives understand the personal value of less expensive approaches to problem solving, acceptance of the AIS™ approach lies in the challenge of improving business performance as a management response to the four components of business success:

- complex challenges of increased global competition;
- need for continually higher profits;
- demand of consumers for improved value in products and services, and
- the psychological contract between workers and managers for an improved quality of life.

Competence stands at the center of the challenge of business performance. Competence is the optimizing factor driving the four components of business success. Hence, I designed the AIS™ to:

1. Meet the challenges of increased global competition by empowering problem- solving methods;
2. Satisfy the need for building consistently higher profits by significantly reducing the cost of coaching, consulting and skills development;
3. Enabling teams and organizations to improve the value of products and services, and
4. Enhancing the psychological contract between employees and managers by improving the quality of life through potent

problem solving.

SMI is aware of the confusion new technology initiatives ignite in the workplace. We understand that such confusion reduces performance on a grand scale. We also recognize that the culprit in this mess remains those technologies, systems, and training programs which erroneously equate knowledge and tools with improved performance while ignoring the formative role of competence in building and maintaining performance. Responding to this plight in the development of competence, SMI advocates a perspective to rapid problem- solving termed Action Learning.

SMI challenges the illusion of the accepted wisdom that knowledge and tools necessarily lead to improved performance, an illusion that ignores the pivotal role of competence in building performance. Our AIS™ approach eliminates the serious problems of mindlessness and coaching confusion associated with previous coaching, consulting and training programs. Through our AIS™ Platform, SMI offers a real, versus apparent, opportunity for improving performance in any organization.

We cannot overstate the critical role of competence in the improvement of enterprise performance. It will increasingly serve as a linking pin to the economic health and success of organizations throughout the 21st Century and beyond. Anyone wishing to successfully participate in the evolving global skills development climate can benefit from the Applied Intuitive Solutions™ vision of SMI, its mission, goals, and strategies. Our Vision, and its focus on competency-based performance, will become second nature to those executives wishing to lead their companies through the 21st Century as serious competitors.

Applied Intuitive Solutions™ encapsulates the response of SMI to the rapidly emerging initiative of Electronic Learning, or E-Learning. I nurtured the SMI rapid problem-solving vision in the knowledge gained from more than 45 years of experience seasoned with advanced academic work in behavioral and management science, education, systems and organization inquiry, clinical and social psychology, business administration, information systems, and the philosophy of science.

Through the consulting practice of SMI, 21st Century leaders and their organizations obtain unique value in their desire to improve performance.

Applied Intuition Solutions™ assist organizations with improve performance by capitalizing on problem solving relationships established through the evolutionary problem-solving practices of SMI. I chose the term "Problem Solving Relationships" for two reasons:

1. Respond to the unique problems of mindlessness in Electronic Learning experienced within the commercial, government, and education industries, and
2. Respond to the understand that competence-based learning occurs virtually through human relationships.

Competence enables performance. Among the components of performance, none is more critical than competence. In many E-Learning transactions, where knowledge and tools guide performance, SMI has found that the arbitrator or mediator of performance in the equation of success is competence. Competence is upheld by four crucial workplace skills:

- mobilize innovation and change,
- communicate well,
- manage self, and
- manage others and tasks.

I cannot over state it: The success formula of knowledge and tools encourages failure and diminishes performance, counter-intuitively, when it ignores competence. As we have discussed, competence is a seminal attribute. Much has been written about it. We require competence because without it, our performance fails. Paraphrasing Aristotle:

> Competence is not a part of performance but is all of performance in its entirety, while incompetence is not a part of failure but is all failure in its entirety. — Aristotle, writing on Justice.

The perspective of SMI leverages the force of competence to reduce weak performance and eliminate failure. Competence enables three dimensions of human life:

1. reality;
2. other people, and
3. oneself.

In the dimension of reality, competence enables a person to perform to his manager's expectation. In the dimension of other people, competence enables a person to perform to the expectations of fellow team members specifically and humanity in general, but only to the extent that a person should respect the legitimate rights of his fellow workers, customers, and stakeholders. In the personal dimension, competence enables a person to perform with proper respect for oneself. In systems psychology, these three aspects of competence become issues of relationships and the self.

In the final analysis, we neither attain competence nor improve performance unless our learning employs the building blocks of success that enable us to better:

(1) Mobilize Innovation and Change,
(2) Communicate Well,
(3) Manage Self, and
(4) Manage Others and Tasks.

A person acting with models and tools, but lacking competence, disrupts the environment, incites chaos, and decreases performance. I urge managers to place competence at the center of their business success formula in the drive to consistently build performance. Knowledge and tools without competence will not move team members beyond their current level of performance.

Lacking the requisite level of competence, clients will fail to mobilize innovation and change and communicate well. SMI recognizes that weakness in these essential core skills reduces rather than builds performance. The level of confusion introduced by a number of training programs leads employees to offer many excuses as justifications for their weak performance. The ensuing upheaval reduces performance while eroding the reservoir of competence already existing in the organization.

The Applied Intuitive Solutions™ of SMI enable anyone connected to the Internet to engage in rapid problem solving, globally, 24 hours a day, seven days a week, while eliminating the cost of coaching and consulting. The AIS™ Platform brings rapid problem solving to the Internet. Through the Internet, our content-rich repository becomes the environment for building the new workplace and social relationships formed through our evidence-based solutions.

The increased competence attained through AIS™ introduces a new and improved success formula. I designed this 21st Century formula to enable clients to build personal and business performance and compete globally by overcoming the illusion which ignores competence as the formative ingredient in performance. While a lot of people talk about competence, I have made it the cornerstone of professional performance.

Thought Break Seven

The evolution of the term competence has an interesting history. Though not in the dictionary, in the practical world people use the word as both a compliment and an insult. For example, at retirement everyone dreads being referred to as competent. You know as in "Old Joe was a competent employee. Let's give him a hand for his 40 years of service before we get back to work". Or, there is the genuine compliment in which you are recognized for having unparalleled competence in the way you saved the day. Here, no one wants you to leave after only two years on the job. You will be sorely missed, but your stock options will help relieve the separation anxiety.

Think about it for a moment. What are the aspects of the person's life that in one case produce an insult and, in the other, generate a deep compliment of the highest order? Obviously if Joe served his company well for 40 years, he has really done something quite commendable.

In 40 years, good ole Joe must have attained quite an impressive reservoir of knowledge about the organization. He was most probably an exceedingly competent person. But it was not enough to avoid the common insult for a job well done. And, after all, we all like our good pets.

Competence in the best sense is an intrinsic factor that allows someone to stand out in the area of performance. It means rising well above the rest at the important historical clock-stopping moment to achieve something significant that benefits not only oneself but also those around you, especially those above you.

Real competence is the stuff of champions.

It is as Gene Kerfoot reasoned: That "good enough" factor of performance or human behavior that carries the day in a specific way that delivers beyond expectation. This does not mean that you are everything to all people in the organization and that you know more than everyone else about everything else and can act on it. It does mean, however, that you acted correctly with the knowledge and skill you had at the time to make an important difference to the organization in a politically correct way. Now this is competence.

Perhaps competence is more than performance. It is perhaps a transcendental attitude. Perhaps competence is an attitude born of commitment to do the best one can in any situation. It does not allow one to coast or hold back. Think about it.

> Competence is a statement one makes by putting oneself fully in the effort with whatever skills, knowledge, adaptability, resilience, gratitude, and generosity one has to offer.

The Competence Trap

Competence is not all bed and roses. It, too, can become counter-intuitive. This may occur whenever people become so competent in their profession that they become glued to them even when the profession becomes extremely unfulfilling. A truly competent person is eager to expand his or her horizons and reach out to find something new. Let's consider the "Bases of Competence".

19: Bases of Competence

Introduction

Agreeing with the Corporate-Higher Education Forum, we also maintain that for too long now colleges and private training organizations have neglected the enduring workplace skills. Since we seek to develop personal and group competence to improve workplace performance, we decided to offer AIS™ that focus on skills mastery in four areas of work-skills specializations which together form the bases of competence. These areas include:

1. Mobilizing Innovation and Change,
2. Managing Self,
3. Communicating Well, and
4. Managing Tasks and Others.

Core Environment of Competence

Competent people enjoy advanced communications capabilities. They also enjoy a wide range of theoretical and practical knowledge. From this foundation, individuals exercise the ability to better analyze, synthesize, and apply new knowledge using judgment and critical valuation skills. This environment of abilities forms the core environment of competence. It consists of the following three components which, along with the bases of competence, form the infrastructure of competence:

1. Foundation of advanced communication abilities and knowledge. These abilities and knowledge consist of reading, writing, reasoning, planning, speaking, organizing, leading, listening, and following, and knowledge consisting of theories, facts, information, methods, ideas, liberal and career knowledge.
2. Framework of intellectual and personal development to improve performance.
3. Abilities to analyze, synthesize, and apply knowledge, and

judgement or value.

Transparent & Authentic AIS™ Architecture

Using an architected solution, our AIS™ informs right action. Our platform requires self-directed end-users to access our solutions to master new concepts and rapidly assess the consequences of their actions. Our AIS™ enable end-users to immediately critique their current and past performance using the AIS™ as a new problem-solving standard. Our solutions become workplace transparent by delivering an authentic and evidence-based experience.

Every AIS™ consists of specially generated content intended to deliver evidence-based solutions to resolve an end-user's workplace situation. These evidence-based solutions are generated from a wide range of solution specific content. Each AIS™ is rooted in workplace scenarios and challenges that relate to problem situations currently requiring resolution.

I designed the AIS™ categories as a framework to resolve several categories of behavioral, contextual, technical, static, dynamic, simple and complex problems. Organization can use our Platform to assist Experiential Learning, Collaborative Learning, Performance-Based Learning, Problem-Based Learning, Evidence-Based Learning and Evolutionary Learning.

Critical Success Factors in SMI Success

Successful companies excel at managing their Critical Success Factors (CSFs). These factors provide unique leverage in the drive to beat the competition. Our CSFs are the building blocks of exceptional performance. For SMI, our CSFs are derived from the delivery of exceptional performance in soft-skills competencies, evidence-based support, and Knowledge Management. We build competence by providing continuous access to real-world Applied Intuitive Solutions™, well throughout solution plans, abundant information-on-demand, workplace authentic content, relevant scenarios and stories, integrated work tasks, and mobile Internet delivery. Our Rapid Solutions Mobile

Platform™ improves employee performance and raise workplace productivity. Our CSFs include:

- Good and Useful Content: Correct, appropriate to the audience, appropriate to the purpose, timely, and enduring.
- Evidence-Based Learning: Content reflects the workplace. End-users identify with the solutions and believe that they reflect the problems in their workplace.
- Substance over Form: We employ multimedia only where it improves skills transfer.
- Insightful Flexibility in Fitting All Situations: We deliver a large range of AIS™ to meet the needs of end-users at every level in the company, operational, tactical, and strategic.
- Mobile End-User Friendly: Technology that eliminates the technological barrier. We provide the rapid problem-solving Platform. You solve problems in your own environment.
- Useful after First Use: You can apply the evidence-based solutions immediately at work for years to come.

Reinforced Problem Solving through Workplace

- Application: Improve coaching and review, Knowledge Management and team building. We deliver a problem solving that eliminates the gap between the problem statement and the solution. Use each AIS™ as a coaching application whenever desired.
- Encourage Management Support: Use the solutions to forge professional relationships that build workplace competence.
- Reduce Cultural Conflicts: Our solutions increase cultural awareness and sensitivity.
- Interesting and Workplace Relevant: Our solutions are authentic and originate in actual workplace application.
- Include Principles of Mindful Learning to Avoid Becoming

Shovelware: We designed our AIS™ Environment Platform programs to enhance intellectual skills using Internet delivery.

- Meet Workplace Relevant Objectives: Our solutions are meaningful and motivate end-users. They are performance oriented and include the why, what, when and how of using the content to improve workplace performance and obtain personal benefits. Our solutions employ a practical implementation model.
- Keep Everything Simple: We intend to remove as much complexity as possible in the AIS™ environment. We simplify the business process wherever possible and acknowledge the feedback of clients.

Critical Failure Factors

While many companies concentrate on managing their CSFs, SMI manages its Critical Failure Factors, our CFFs. We realize that our CFFs complement our CSFs. Our CFFs include:

- Delivering Poor, Boring and/or Inappropriate Solutions: f our content fails, SMI cannot be a leading Rapid Solutions Institute. We need to adhere to the principles of Mindful Learning.
- Using Inconsistent and Unfair Business Practices: We cannot fail to support all clients and with consistently fair service and pricing. We will discount prices where discounts are possible. We will always try to offer the lowest possible price. We will offer everyday low pricing.
- Use an Ineffective Problem-Solving Architecture: Online solution delivery is inappropriate for some situations. Effective solution architectures resolve this weakness. Some problem solving is better suited for an interpersonal and interactive work setting. Not everything should be delivered

on the Internet.

- Favor Presentation over Content: Although we may be tempted to add an abundance of multimedia attractiveness, we will use multimedia in our solutions only when it facilitates problem solving and improves the value of the content.
- Use Subject Matter Experts (SME) as Technical Writers: Preparing content for online delivery is time consuming. Not every expert can do it comfortably. Moreover, we question if we want to employ such expensive resources to tasks that can be better done by others. It is more reasonable to employ SMEs in the rapid transfer of intellectual property. We also understand that preparing online solutions is very different from facilitating in-class instruction. The skills, experience, and abilities required to succeed in the development of online rapid problem solving differ greatly from those of in-class teaching. Not every expert has what it takes to develop solutions for online problem solving.
- Use Technical Writers as Content Authors: A technical writer is a technical writer, and can be an expert in it. Generally, an SME is an expert in a strategic, operational, tactical, and/or technical domain. SMEs know a lot about a specific field of expertise. Sometimes they can teach others their expertise. A technical writer generally does not enjoy such expertise. Today, with the rapid acceptance of online learning, a few technical writers unwisely market themselves as SMEs in almost every area of expertise. Technical writing is far different from serving as an SME. The two should not be confused. Using SMEs as technical writers weakens the value proposition of Rapid Problem Solving.
- Confuse Theory with Practice: We want our solutions to remain authentic and relevant. Thus, our programs are action

oriented rather than theoretical. While we may link theory with practice to improve the content, we cannot lose track of our desire to improve workplace performance by offering authentic solutions and problem-solving models.

- Confuse the Need for Information with the Need for Solutions: This is all about balance and value. Whenever we use content as reference information, we fail our client. Some knowledge is more appropriately learned through documentation, models, reference materials, and information. Solutions are unnecessarily costly and time consuming. Remember, competence is about knowledge, proficiency is about experience.
- Offering Content that Fails to Improve Learner and Business Performance - Whenever we offer inauthentic content that lacks intrinsic or extrinsic workplace value, we fail the client and ourselves.

Conflict the Culture: Our AIS™ must support the client need and improve the performance of the organization culture. Our solutions:

1. Link all problem solving with work;
2. Focus at the enterprise level strategically;
3. Raise the value of knowledge;
4. Emphasize both competence and performance;
5. Encourage an open culture of problem solving
6. and skills acquisition;
7. Minimize costs and other barriers;
8. Facilitate friendly learning access, and
9. Certify solutions.

A carefully designed problem-solving architecture establishes the skills acquisition in its proper relation to rapid problem solving. It details the path to the enhancement of competence and improvement of workplace performance through enhanced employee proficiency.

20: Conclusion to Part Two

Part Two prepared readers for Part Three by discussing several closely related formative concepts of competence that point the way to the Ulthule™ approach to Peak Performance, this approach prepares us to attack the challenge of linking performance to competence within the ethical dimension of the Evolutionary Guidance System. Later this will guide us through the evolutionary design project that enables us to better achieve the mission of the SMI Design Inquiry Human Activity System.

Glossary

Appreciative System: A Human Activity System in which the guiding principle acknowledges the intrinsic value of human beings as the most valuable components of a goal directed and dynamic system.

Automatic Invoice Reconciliation (AIR): A management method that employs Information Technologies to reconcile invoices on the spot as shipments arrive at customer sites and generate payments immediately without invoices. This method eliminates the need for submitting invoices and waiting on remittances. AIR significantly improves cash flows and reduces business processes.

Behavior Theory of Leadership: Refers to a theory of leadership in which mere action connotes leadership. Leadership is what a leader does. Without success, there can be no leadership. Success and leadership are synonymous.

Business Intelligence Group (BIG): This is the postmodern model for information gathering, management and dissemination. It replaces the Management Information Services function with an executive-centric information model and an on-line, real-time information movement paradigm.

CATWOE: Refers to the components of a system description including the customers, actors, transformations, weltanschauung, owners, and environment.

Chief Enterprise Architect (CEA): This person understands postmodern strategy and the power of Information Technology to leverage that strategy. The CEA balances strategy, Information Technology, business ecosystems, and the value chain of customer satisfaction to disrupt the business environment to attain competitive leverage. This executive may be the CEO, the CIO or the COO. (S)he understands the new 7-S model of business growth.

Chief Executive Officer (CEO): The most senior managing executive in an organization; guides the EGS and reports to the Chairperson of the Board.

Chief Financial Officer (CFO): The most senior financial executive in an organization; also, the comptroller or treasurer.

Chief Information Officer (CIO): This position replaces the Director of Information Systems; leads the development of the Strategic Information Systems Architecture; employs Information Technologies to empower the business plan; employs technology to provide competitive leverage; provide the information systems vision to the enterprise. Serves as the enterprise ecologist and chief business intelligence officer.

Client Server Computing (CSC): A model of I/T implementation in which information is distributed throughout the enterprise using a real-time approach. CSC accommodates information distribution and management centralization. CSC signifies a major shift in management philosophy in that executives now see Information Technology as an enabler of decision making rather than as a supporter of management control.

Competitive Leverage: Refers to the strategy of employing Information Technology to attain hypergrowth, generate disruption in the market, and dominate the business ecosystem.

Computer Aided Design (CAD): Refers to the use of computers to improve the technical design process; CAD employs computers to enhance the production of design documents.

Computer Aided Manufacturing (CAM): Refers to the use of computers to empower manufacturing operations.

Computer Integrated Manufacturing (CIM): Refers to the use of computers to enhance the profitability of manufacturing operations by integrating specific manufacturing tasks and reducing non-valued added activities.

Cyber Security (CS): Cybersecurity refers to the processes and systems designed to protect internet-connected systems and their components and data from computer and network attacks to cause damage, destruction, theft, and/or unauthorized access. It consists of specific social and technical procedures, processes, measures, policies, systems and technologies crafted to block and defeat cyber-attacks. They maintain confidentiality of systems data and information, prevention unauthorized systems access and intrusions. Their goal is to maintain security, availability, integrity and confidentiality of systems, data, and information, the CIA.

Decision Support Systems (DSS): Refers to the use of computers and Information Technologies to enhance repetitive decision making usually at the operational management level.

Design Inquiry: Refers to the systems method of designing human activity systems models in which the designer leverages certain system dynamics to progress through the spaces, environments, and systems of design.

Design Solution Space: Refers to the conceptual space in which the design takes shape. It is the work space in which the human activity system design Working identifies the purposes and goals of the design by engaging in the interactive dynamics of design. The Reproducer Subsystem functions in this space.

Design System: Refers to the human activity system that produces the new HAS in respect to the ideal systems models developed by the value system as a product of the meta-system. This HAS works in the domains of description, vocabulary, knowledge, and interpretations to engage in design. The Design System conducts the design inquiry and interacts with the knowledge system to obtain knowledge about generating the action sequences of design. It engages in design inquiry.

Design Support System: Using management and maintenance activities, this system energizes the Design System to manage the design inquiry and maintain itself as it designs the Ideal System.

Deterministic System: Having externally set goals to meet prescribed operational objectives, this type of human se activity system selects its own method of operating.

Direct Business Practices (DBP): Refers to a family of business practices and management approaches designed to reduce the cost of inventory management, shipping, and procurement business practices.

Direct Store Delivery (DSD): DSD is a direct business practice in which a supplier ships a product directly to the customer immediately from production rather than through a Distribution Center, warehouse or through a broker.

Dynamics of Divergence and Convergence: While divergence tends towards systems evolution to produce quantitative equalization, convergence results from a similarly directed selection on the part of a similar environment.

Dynamics of Feedback and Feedforward: Refers to the dynamics through which designers discern the iterative requirements of design by going back and forth within the environments of design to discern the design requirements.

Dynamics of Interactive and Spiralic Design: Refers to the process through which designers progressively visit and revisit the conceptual spaces of design until the new design of the human activity system emerges.

Dynamics of Multi-Systemic Thrust in Design: Refers to the process in which designer coordinate and refine preliminary designs throughout the design architecture in considering every expediency of design.

Dynamics of Participative Design: Refers to the process through which designers engage the exploratory and issues resolution cycles of design to ensure that they examine the information of the design and listen to all comments.

Effective Business Relationships (EBR): Refers to the management practice of doing the right thing right to attain profitable business relationships; it overcomes the weaknesses of efficiency in which an organization may do the wrong thing right to attain growth without profits.

Efficient Consumer Response (ECR): Refers to a group of management practices employed in the grocery industry to reduce the cost of products to consumers; ECR consists of several distinct phases of implementation; it is empowered by Information Technology.

Efficient Product Categories: Refers to the ECR practice of managing products by category to maximize profits per category.

Efficient Product Introductions: Refers to the ECR practice of using Information Technology to reduce the cost of product failures.

Efficient Promotions: Refers to the ECR practice of using Information Technology to obtain improved customer loyalty.

Efficient Replenishment: Refers to the ECR approach of employing Information Technology along the supply chain to reduce the cost of replenishment.

Electronic Commerce (EC): Refers to the executive strategy to employ Information Technology to attain efficient business operations and hypergrowth.

Electronic Commerce-Distributed Business Practices (EC-DBP): Refers to the management practice of employing Information Technology to empower Distributed Business Practices under centralized control.

Electronic Document Interchange (EDI): Refers to the use of Information Technology to send and receive common business documents in a standardized format; EDI includes the data and the formats that forms the business documents.

Electronic Funds Transfer (EFT): Refers to the use of EDI to transmit cash and the accompanying business documents.

Electronic Learning: Refers to an education and/or training approach in which learning content is made available twenty-four hours a day, seven days a week through the internet.

Enterprise Architecture Planning (EAP): A type of management planning which is designed to link business plans and Information Systems; it provides an enterprise-wide information architecture.

Enterprise Intelligence Officer (EIO) is the enterprise ecologist who carefully examines strategic consequences of Cyber Security. The EIO works with the Chief Executive Officer to replace forecasting with Cyber Security scenario setting as an appropriate response to the new environments protected through Cyber Security

Enterprise Resource Planning (ERP): Involves the use of Information Technology to manage all the activities of an enterprise in an integrated fashion.

Enterprise Requirements Planning (ERP): Similar to Enterprise Resource Planning above with the addition of scenario building and requirements planning.

Environments of Design: Refers to the environment in which human activity systems design occurs. These are the Environment of the System of Ideals/Aspirations/Intentions/ Problems, Environment of the Future System, Environment of the Design System, and Knowledge Environment.

Environment of the Design System: By cycling from the conceptual world to the physical, this system provides all the matter, energy and information required for design. The design HAS works within this environment using the models of the design system that will become a concrete system during design.

Environment of the Future System: Refers to the design environment that serves as a conceptual source of inputs for the HAS to be designed. This Environment contains the models of the future system and is the environment in which the new HAS comes to reside.

Environment of the System of Ideas, Aspirations, Intentions, and Problems: Refers to the conceptual environment that represents the environment of the dynamic system of organizing perspectives. This environment forms the conceptual space of the system of problems and consists of: (a) the concrete, currently existing human activity system; (b) a model of the new human activity system; © the models of the objectives and goals of the new human activity system in the form of structural models, and (d) the system of intentions or values such as improved performance which ignited the idea to redesign the human activity system for e-commerce.

Evolutionary Guidance System (EGS): Refers to a type of Human Activity System in which the components are continually evolving toward evolutionary consciousness; the components of an EGS seek evolutionary competence.

Executive Information Systems (EIS): Similar to DSS but used at the executive level to improve tactical level decision making.

Experience Space: Refers to the conceptual design in which designers test alternative models against reality. The Experience Space includes the environments and systems of design specific to the knowledge base systems, the existing Human Activity Systems, the support systems, and the design inquiry system. Value systems design occurs in the experience space.

Heuristic System: Refers to human activity systems which emerge new structures and relational networks through time. Emergence, ambiguity, high levels of uncertainty, evolution and design characterize these systems. Changes in state common to heuristics systems are driven by design more than random evolution. They are complex open systems that co-evolve with their environments and display systemic structures as they formulate their own goals and objectives to respond to their well-defined purpose.

Horizontal Management (also Process Perspective): Refers to the shift in executive thinking and management practice in which the business is viewed as a system of interdependent core business processes supporting a value chain. Horizontal Management replaces the traditional view of an enterprise as a group of business functions or vertical operations such as marketing and manufacturing. Executives view order generation, replenishment, product introduction, and so forth as core business processes for their companies. This view requires a strategic Information Technology architecture as a framework for success. This view employs I/T to leverage competitive business practices. Since Horizontal Management employs I/T to "empower" business productivity and competitive performance, it requires a strategic I/T vision to enable an appropriate design of the core business processes.

Human Activity System (HAS): This is a system in which the components are human beings; it is a goal-directed, system in which the human beings share a common purpose.

Human Resource Information Systems (HRIS): Refers to an Information System designed to support the activities of Human Resources Management; can be either a simple or complex computer system with many modules.

Hypercompetition: Refers to a form of competition that seeks growth rather than harvesting; Hypercompetition is characterized by disruption and a new "7-S" model of competition; Hypercompetition replaces Sustaining Competitive Advantage as a new management model.

Hypergrowth: Refers to the business phenomena succeeding well enough in business to achieve a billion dollars of revenue in five years or less; Hypergrowth employs Hypercompetition as a business strategy.

Hyper-System Definition: Refers to the process of building a KITWE description for the all-inclusive system consisting of the systems within the narrow and wider environments of interest.

Incremental Rate of Return (IRR): In post-modern business operations, IRR refers to the enhanced ROI made possible through the use of modern Information Technologies.

Information Movement and Management (IM&M): Refers to the methods, processes, models and standards which enables CSC; IM&M employs I/T to empower CSC.

Information Technology (I/T): Refers to the computer hardware, software, networks, and communications connections that move and management information; I/T is the enabler of CSC.

Interaction Dynamics of Design: Refers to the iterative systems Dynamics of Feedback and Feedforward, Interactive and Spiralic Design, Divergence and Convergence, Multi-Systemic Thrust in Design, and Participative Design.

International Standards Organization (ISO): Refers to an international group of experts that define numerous types of standards for business and government such as ISO9003 for quality certification in Information Systems Management.

Just-In-Time (JIT): Refers to a management approach to inventory management that is triggered by demand; it is a pull system of production rather than a push system.

Knowledge Environment: Refers to the environment which provides the inputs required to formulate the Knowledge Base System as an abstract system. It contains the entire knowledge stock relevant to design as a disciplined inquiry (Banathy, 1984).

Knowledge Space: Refers to the conceptual space which serves as the repository of the design process. It contains all the knowledge explored during design inquiry, including the specific, generic and general design knowledge.

Knowledge System: Refers to the conceptual system that provides all knowledge relevant to design process. This System provides input to the Design System to energize the System of Operations within the Problem Solution Space.

Leadership Support Systems (LSS): Refers to an EGS that supports the evolutionary unfolding of an enterprise; an LSS is an Appreciative HAS.

Logistics Management Institute (LMI): Refers to a private enterprise that engages in Logistics Management Research & Development.

Management Information Systems (MIS): Refers to the traditional model of Information Systems through which organizations employ computers to provide batch processing and management reporting as input to the decision-making process. In this view MIS support the communications and control functions of management.

Material Requirements Planning (MRP): Refers to the use of Information Technology to support material planning and forecasting.

Material Resources Planning (MRPII): Refers to the expansion of MRP to include enterprise-wide resources planning.

Materials Tracking & Control (MT&C): Refers to a group of management methods and computer systems that improve the shop floor control and routing of materials.

Metamethodology: Refers to a methodology for designing methodologies.

Meta-Systems Design: Refers to the design of the system that designs systems.

Methodology: Refers to the repository of tools and techniques appropriate to a specific type of problem. Methodologies must be specific to a particular type3 of program and system type to be relevant.

On-Line Analytical Processing (OLAP): Refers to emerging computer-based technologies that empower operational and tactical level management decision making. OLAP refers to an approach to DSS and EIS based on multi-dimensional, statistical analysis and reporting.

Paradigm Shift: Refers to the shift in thinking that transforms an enterprise into a system of core business processes. The current paradigm shift views an enterprise as a system of interdependent horizontal business processes rather than as a collection of functional departments.

Participative Management: Refers to the management practice of sharing targeted decisions, roles and responsibilities with employees.

Point-Of-Sale (POS): Refers to the use of Information Technology to capture a wide range of business information at the points-of-sale; organizations may use POS information to engage in Vendor Managed Replenishment, inventory management, promotions management, and so forth.

Problem or Contextual Space: Refers to the conceptual space which contains all the sources employed in defining, studying, and characterizing all the problems, values and systems relevant to the design project (Banathy, 1984). The Contextual Space includes the environments and systems of design specific to the problem context and the existing Human Activity System or HAS. Meta-systems design and hyper-system definition occur in this design space.

Process Management: Refers to the horizontal or process-oriented management paradigm describes above. This view requires a strategic Information Technology architecture as a framework for success.

Purpose Seeking System: Highly autonomous human activity system that provides its own goals, objects, and methods of behavior. This system is fully capable of seeking its own self-transcendence.

Purposive System: Refer to the type of human activity system that mark the mid-point of the continuum. They enjoy heightened interactions with the environment and selects its own operational objectives, methods and means of operations. These systems may also embed deterministic and rigidly controlled systems.

Quick Response (QR): Refers to a management strategy used by the general merchandising industry for improving the efficiency of business process. QR was the model used by the grocery to design ECR; it is an enterprise-wide Information Technology empowered business model.

Rigidly Controlled System: Refers to a human activity system that obtains goals, objectives, and rules from the external environment. This system does not engage in self-direction.

Spaces of Design: Refers to the conceptual spaces traversed during design inquiry. These spaces are Design Solution Space, Knowledge Space, Problem or Contextual Space, and Experience Space.

Sustaining Competitive Advantage (SCA): Refers to the traditional management myth that one company can indefinitely maintain a competitive advantage over business rivals; it is an elaborate business model which includes an impressive formula which employs a specific type of "7-S" model based on the harvest strategy.

Systems Engineering Method (SEM): Refers to a disciplined method of expanding a problem domain to discover counter-intuitive solutions; employs expansionism rather than reductionism as a philosophical basis.

Systems of Design: Refers to the systems engaged during design inquiry to model a human activity system. These systems are the System of Problems, System to be Designed, Design System, Systems of Operations, Knowledge System, and the Design Support System.

System of Operations: Refers to the conceptual system that activates or enables the operations required to initiate the systems design methodology. It energizes the other systems in the Problem Solution Space.

System of Problems: Refers to the conceptual system that focuses on the problem context, including the existing problems in the existing HAS, such as the failure to define normative categories for e-commerce strategy selection.

System to be Designed: Refers to the conceptual system that focuses on the ideal system that is to be designed as the future HAS.

Theory of Human Activity Systems Types: Refers to the continuum of human activity systems ranging from rigidly controlled to the self-transcending human activity systems. The systems types are Rigidly Controlled Systems, Deterministic Systems, Purposive Systems, Heuristic Systems, Purpose Seeking Systems.

Trait Theory of Leadership: Refers to the theory in which leadership is a function of special personality or psychological traits such as resilience, adaptability, intelligence, and so forth.

UlThule™ Performance: Refers to the attainment of human performance at the highest level possible. Contraction from the two Latin words Ultima and Thule, the highest point.

Value Added Network (VAN): Refers to a vendor or other third party who provides EDI or other EC business document translation or mail box services.

Value System: Refers to that system which contains all the formative values which include the design of a future human activity system.

Vendor Managed Replenishment (VMR): A management approach, empowered by Information Technology, through which vendors manage the inventory and replenishment cycles of prime customers.

Virtual Commerce (VC): Refers to the state of business operations in which management employs Information Technology coupled with efficient business practices to attain virtual business operations globally 24 hours a day, seven days a week.

Vision: Refers to the organizing perspective of human objectives, goals, plans, and designs. The vision is that which drives action to some end at the over-arching level.

Vision 21: A strategic action tool of the Systems Management Institute designed to reduce the hidden cost and risk inherent in adopting new business strategies.

Winning Production (WP): Refers to a management approach of using a specific set of management practices as requirements for success such as balancing inventory to improve manufacturing operations.

References

Ackoff, Russell L. (1981). Creating the Corporate Future. New York, New York: John Wiley & Sons.

Ackoff, R.L., & Emery, Fred E. (1972). On Purposeful Systems. Seaside, CA: Intersystems Publications.

Agresti, W.W. (1986). New Paradigms for Software Development. Washington, D.C: IEEE Computer

Society Press.

Andriole, Stephen J. (1986). Microcomputer Decision Support Systems: Design, Implementation and Evaluation. Wellesley, Mass: QED Information Sciences, Inc.

Arthur, Lowell Jay (1985). Measuring Programmer

Productivity and Software Quality. New York, New York: John Wiley & Sons.

——(1988). Software Evolution: The Software Maintenance Challenge. New York, New York: John Wiley & Sons.

Bakker, B.H. (1979). Model Building, mathematical techniques and data analysis. In B. A. Bayraktar, H. Muller-Merbach, J. E. Roberts, and M. E. Simpson (Eds.), Education in system science. New York: Halstead Press.

Banathy, Bela (1973). Developing a Systems View of Education. Seaside, CA: Intersystems Publications.

——(1979). Introduction to Systems Inquiry. Seaside, California: Intersystems Publishers.

——(1983). Systems behavior. San Francisco: Saybrook Institute.

——(1984). Systems Design in the Context of Human Activity Systems. San Francisco, CA: International Systems Institute.

——(1986). The Design of Design Inquiry in the Context of Human Activity Systems. San Francisco, CA: Far West Laboratory for Educational Research and Development.

——(1987a). Human Systems Inquiry Course Guide, Appendix A. San Francisco, CA: Saybrook Institute.

——(1987c). The Design of Evolutionary Guidance Systems. San Francisco, CA: Saybrook Institute.

——(1987b). The Characteristics and Acquisition of Evolutionary Competence. From World Futures, Vol. 23, pp. 123-144. Gordon and Breach Science

Publishers, Inc.

——(1988). Matching Design Methods to System Type. San Francisco: CA: Saybrook Institute.

——(1989). Design: A Journey to Create the Future as a Map of the Journey. Carmel, CA: Far West Laboratory and Saybrook Institute.

Bateson, G. (1979). Mind And Nature: A Necessary Unity. New York, NewYork: Bantam Books.

Beizer, Boris (1984). Software System Testing and Quality Assurance. New York, New York: Van Nostrand Reinhold Company.

Bielawski, Larry & Lewand, Robert (1991). Intelligent Systems Design: Integrating Expert Systems, Hypermedia, and Database Technologies. New York: John Wiley & Sons.

Boar, Bernard H. (1993). Implementing client/server computing: A strategic perspective. New York: McGraw-Hill, Inc.

Bogdanov, A. (1984). Essays in Tektology the General Science of Organization. Seaside, California: Intersystems Publications.

Bouldin, Barbara M. (1989). Agents of Change. Englewood Cliffs, New Jersey: Prentice Hall.

Branden, Nathaniel (1974). The Psychology of SelfEsteem. New York, New York: Bantam Books.

Burrell, G. & Morgan, G. (1979). Sociological Paradigms and Organizational Analysis. London: Heinemann.

Burstein, Daniel (1990). "Engineering the New Europe." A conversation with Jacques Delors, U.S. Air Inflight Magazine, January, 1990, p. 74.

Carrico, Michael A., Girard, John E., & Jones, Jennifer P. (1989). Building Knowledge Systems. New York, New York: McGraw-Hill Book Company.

Cavallo, R. E. (Ed.) (1979, July). Systems research movement: Characteristics, accomplishments, and current developments. Binghampton, NY: Society for General Systems Research.

Checkland, Peter (1981). Systems Thinking, Systems Practice. New York, New York: John Wiley & Sons.

Cho, Chin-Kuei (1987). Quality Programming: Developing And Testing Software With Statistical Quality Control. New York, New York: John Wiley &

Sons.

Churchman, C.W. (1971). The Design of Inquiring Systems. New York, New York: Basic Books.

——(1979). The Systems Approach. New York, New

York: Laurel.

Collen, Arne (1985). "Experimental Method Within Systems Methodology: The Case for and Against", B. Banathy, editor. Proceeding of the Society for General Systems Research, pp. 536-539, Vol. 1. Seaside, California: Intersystems Publishers.

Copleston, S.J., F. (1985). A History of Philosophy, Vol. 1. New York, New York: Doubleday.

Coyne, R.D., Rosenman, M.A., Radford, A.D., Balachandran, M., Gero, J.S.(1990). Knowledge-Based Design Systems. New York, New York: AddisonWesley Publishing Company.

Dawson, Dorr (1990). "A Conversation About Management," from a private meeting. Walnut Creek, California: Unpublished Comments.

DeMarco, Tom (1982). Controlling Software Projects. New York, New York: Yourdon Press.

DeMillo, McCracken, Martin, Passafiume (1987).

Software Testing and Evaluation. Menlo Park, CA: The Benjamin Cummings Publishing Company, Inc.

Dickinson, Brian (1980). Developing Structured Systems: A Methodology Using Structured Techniques.

New York, New York: Yourdon Press.

——(1989). Developing Quality Systems: A Methodology Using Structured Techniques. New York, New York: McGraw-Hill Book Company.

Dinsmore, Paul C. (1984). Human Factors in Project Management. New York, New York: American Management Association Publications Group.

Drucker, Peter F. (1989). The New Realties. New York, New York: Harper &Row, Publishers.

Dunn, Robert & Ullman, Richard (1982). Quality

Assurance for Computer Software. New York, New York: McGraw-Hill Book Company.

Evans, Michael W. (1984). Product Software Test Management. New York, New York: John Wiley & Sons.

Evans, Michael W. & Marciniak, John J. (1987). Software Quality Assurance & Management. New York, New York: John Wiley & Sons, Inc.

Fisher, Alan S. (1988). CASE: Using Software Development Tools. New York, New York: John Wiley & Sons.

Flood, Robert L. & Carson, Ewart R. (1988). Dealing With Complexity. New York, New York: Plenum Press.

Florian, M. (1974). On the teaching of model building: Mathematical techniques and data analysis. B. A. Bayraktar, H. Muller-Merbach, J. E. Roberts, and

M. G. Simpson (Eds.), Education in systems science. New York: Halsted Press.

Foerster, Heinz von (1984). Observing Systems. Seaside, California: Intersystems Publications.

Fournier, Roger (1991). Practical Guide to Structured System Development and Maintenance. Englewood Cliffs, New Jersey: Yourdon Press.

Gane, Chris (1989). Rapid System Development: Using Structured Techniques and Relational Technology. Englewood Cliffs, New Jersey: Prentice Hall.

Gasparski, W. (1984). Understanding Design: The Praxiological Systemic Perspective. Seaside, CA: Intersystems Publishers.

Gause, G.G., Weinberg, G.M. (1989). Exploring Requirements: Quality Before Design. New York, New York: Dorset House Publishing.

Gigch van, J.P. (1989). The Well-Being of Organizations, edited by C. West Churchman. Seaside, CA: Intersystems Publications.

Gilbreath, Robert D. (1986). Winning at Project Management. New York, New York: John Wiley & Sons.

Goldstein, Martin & Goldstein, Inge (1978). How We Know: An Exploration of the Scientific Process. New York, New York: Plenum Press.

Grady, Robert B. & Caswell, Deborah L. (1987). Software Metrics: Establishing a Company-Wide Program. Englewood Cliffs, New Jersey: Prentice Hall.

Grejner, K.L. (1963). Electric Devices Design Methodology Foundations. ref. by Gasparski (1984). Moscow: Gosenergoizdat.

Gugliotti, J.A. & Crescenzi, A.D. (1990). "The Portfolio Approach to Systems Development," from The Handbook of Systems Management Development and Support, 1990-1991 Yearbook, Ed. Paul C. Tinnirello. New York, New York: Auerbach Publishers.

Hanneman, G. J. (1975). Models and model building in communication research. G. J. Hanneman, et al. (Eds.), Communication in behavior. New York: Addison-Wesley.

Hickey, Jack (1973). "Discussion on Philosophy," from a private meeting. Dayton, Ohio: Sinclair Community College.

Jackson, M. C. (1987). "New Directions In Management Science." In Jackson, M.C., and Keys, P. (eds.), New Dimensions in Management Science. Aldershot: Gower.

Jackson, M.C., & Keys, P. (1984). "Towards a system of systems methodologies," Journal of the Operations Research Society, 35(6), pp. 473-486.

Jantsch, E. & Waddington, C.H. (1976). Evolution and Consciousness: Human Systems in Transition. Reading, Mass: Wiley.

Joint Industry Committee on Deductions (1990). Invoice Deductions Guidelines, Executive Summary. Washington DC: Research Department, Food Marketing Institute.

Joint Industry Project on Efficient Consumer Response (1994). Performance Measurement, Applying Value Chain Analysis to the Grocery Industry. Washington DC: Food Marketing Institute.

Jones, J.C. (1970). Design Methods. New York, New York: Wiley.

Katsenelinboigen, Aron (1989). Selected Topics in Indeterministic Systems. Seaside, California: Intersystems Publications.

Kerr, Edwin F. (1989). CASE: The Potential and the Pitfalls. Wellesley, Mass: Q.E.D. Information Sciences.

Kerzner, Harold (1989). Project Management: A Systems Approach to Planning, Scheduling, and Controlling. New York, New York: Van Nostrand Reinhold.

Klir, G. (1985). Architecture of Systems Problem Solving. New York, New York: Plenum Press.

Kotarbinski, T. (1966). Gnosiology: The Scientific Approach to the Theory of Knowledge. Oxford, England: Pergamon Press.

Kremer, J. W. (1986). "The human science approach as discourse." The Saybrook review, 6 (1). Spring, pp. 65-106.

Kuhn, T.S. (1970). The Structure of Scientific Revolutions. Chicago, Ill: University of Chicago Press.

Kurt Salmon Associates, Inc. Management Consultants (1993). Efficient Consumer Response, Enhancing Consumer Value in the Grocery Industry. Washington, DC: Research Department, Food Marketing Institute.

Langer, Ellen, J. (1989). Mindfulness. Reading, Mass: Perseus Books.

Lantz, Kenneth E. (1987). The Prototyping Methodology. Englewood Cliffs, New Jersey: Prentice-Hall.

Levinson, Eliot (1984). The Implementation of Executive Support Systems, working paper 3119, Center for Information Systems Research, Sloan School of Management, MIT, Cambridge, Mass., October, 1984.

Lippitt, G. L. (1973). Visualizing changes. La Jolla, CA: University Associates.

Management Research Group (1992). Leadership Effectiveness Analysis. Portland, Maine: Management Research Group.

Martin, James (1987). Recommended Diagramming Standards for Analysts &Programmers: A Basis for Automation. Englewood Cliffs, New Jersey: Prentice-Hall, Inc.

——(1990). Information Engineering Design & Construction. Englewood Cliffs, New Jersey: Prentice Hall.

Martin, James & Oxman, Steven (1988). Building Expert Systems. Englewood Cliffs, New Jersey: Prentice Hall.

McClure, Carma (1989). CASE IS Software Automation. Englewood Cliffs, New Jersey: Prentice Hall.

McKerrow, Phillip (1987). Performance Measurement of Computer Systems. New York, New York: McGraw-Hill.

McMillan, Grant R., Beevis, David, Salas, Eduardo, Strub, Michael H., Sutton, Robert, & Van Breda, Leo (1989). Applications of human performance models to system design. New York: Plenum Press.

Mercer, Michael (1989). Turning Your Human Resources Department into a Profit Center. New York, New York: AMACOM, American Management Association.

Miller, James G. (1987). Living Systems. New York, New York: McGraw Hill Book Company.

Misiak, Henryk & Sexton, Virginia S. (1966). History of Psychology. New York, New York: Grune.

Moore, James F. (1996). The Death of Competition: Leadership and Strategy in the Age of Business Ecosystems. New York, New York: Harper Collins.

Myers, Glenford J. (1979). The Art of Software Testing. New York, New York: John Wiley & Sons, Inc.

Naughton, J. (1977). The Checkland Methodology: A Readers Guide. (2nd ed.). Milton Keynes: Open University Press.

Nemoto, Masao (1987). Total Quality Control for Management: Strategies and Techniques from Toyota and Toyoda Gosei. Englewood Cliffs, New Jersey:

Prentice-Hall, Inc.

Newkirk, Raymond L. (1976). The Descent of Man. unpublished manuscript. New York, New York: New York Institute of Technology.

———-(1982). The Chronicles of the Making of a Philosopher, Book II, What is Philosophy? (Master Thesis). Mill Valley, CA: Columbia

Pacific University.

——(1987). Letter to the Filipino People. from letter written to her Excellency Cory Aquino, President of the Philippine Republic.

——(1988). A Deductive Process Model of The Computer Software Development Human Activity System. Pleasant Hill, California: Saybrook Institute (Academic Paper).

——(1989). The Living Systems Approach: A New Software Design Paradigm for the 21st Century and Beyond. Pleasant Hill, California: Saybrook Institute (Academic Manuscript).

——(1990). Design Evaluation and Measurement: Evolutionary Guidance System. (Academic Manuscript). San Francisco, CA: Saybrook Institute.

——(1991). Systems Management Beyond Project Management. Pleasant Hill, California: Saybrook Institute (Academic Manuscript).

Olle, Hagelstein, Macdonald, Rolland, Sol, Van Assche, Verrijn-Stuart (1988). Information Systems Methodologies: A Framework for Understanding.

Menlo Park, California: Addison-Wesley.

Orr, Ken (1981). Structured Requirements Definition. Topeka, Kansas: Ken Orr and Associates, Inc.

Page-Jones, Meilir (1980). The Practical Guide to Structured Systems Design. New York, New York: Yourdon Press.

——(1985). Practical Project Management: Restoring Quality to DP Projects and Systems. New York, New York: Dorset House Publishing.

Parsave, Chignell, Khoshafian & Wong (1989). Intelligent Databases: Object Oriented, Deductive Hypermedia Technologies. New York, New York: John Wiley & Sons.

Perry, W. E. (1982). Hatching The EDP Quality Assurance Function. Wellesley, MA: Q.E.D. Information Sciences, Inc.

——(1983). A Structured Approach to Systems Testing. Wellesley, Mass: Q.E.D. Information Sciences, Inc.

——(1987a). Effective Methods of EDP Quality Assurance. Wellesley, Mass: Q.E.D. Information Sciences, Inc.

——(1987b). A Standard for Testing Application Software. Boston, Mass: Auerbach Publishers, Inc.

Petrie, H.G. (1968)."The Strategy Sense of Methodology." Philosophy of Science, pp. 248-257.

Plunkett, Lorne C. & Fournier, Robert (1991). Participative Management: Implementing Empowerment. New York, New York: John Wiley & Sons.

Polkinghorne, Donald (1983). Methodology for the Human Sciences: Systems of Inquiry. Albany, New York: State University of New York Press.

Powers, Pat (1984). Methodological Issues. San Francisco, CA: Saybrook Institute (Unpublished Essay).

Prigogine, I. (1976). "Order through fluctuation: Self-organization and social systems," Jantsch, E. & Waddington, C. H. (Eds.). Evolution and consciousness: Human systems in transitions. Reading, MA: Addison-Wesley Publishing Company.

Ramamoorthy, C.V., Usuda, Y., Prakash, A., & Tsai, W.T. (1990). "The Evolution Support Environment." IEEE Transactions on Software Engineering, Vol. 16, No. 11, pp. 1225-1235.

Reckmeyer, W.J. (1982). The Emerging Systems Paradigm: An Historical Perspective. Washington, D.C: The American University (Unpublished Doctoral
Dissertation).

Rockart & Bullen (1986). The Rise of Managerial Computing. Homewood Illinois: Dow Jones-Irwin.

Rockart & DeLong (1988). Executive Support Systems: The Emergence of Top Management Computer Use. Homewood, Illinois: Dow Jones-Irwin.

Roetzheim, William H. (1988). Structured Computer Project Management. Englewood Cliffs, New Jersey: Prentice-Hall.

——(1991). Developing Software to Government Standards. Englewood Cliffs, New Jersey: Prentice Hall.

Rosenau, Milton D., Jr. (1981). Successful Project Management: A Step-by-Step Approach with Practical Examples. New York, New York; Van Nostrand Reinhold.

Schindler, Max (1990). Computer-Aided Software Design: Build Quality Software with CASE. New York, New York: John Wiley & Sons.

Schulmeyer, G. Gordon (1990). Zero Defect Software. New York, New York: McGraw-Hill, Inc.

Schulmeyer, G. Gordon & McManus, James I. (1987). Handbook Of Software Quality Assurance. New York, New York: Van Nostrand Reinhold.

Security Pacific Automation Corporation. (1989). ADS/se Software Engineering Methodology. Los Angeles, California: Security Pacific Automation Company.

Senge, Peter M. (1990). The Fifth Discipline. New York, N. Y: Doubleday.

Simon, Hebert A. (1969). The Sciences of the Artificial. Cambridge, Mass: MIT Press.

Stamps, Jeffrey S. (1980). Holonomy: A Human Systems Theory. Seaside, California: Intersystems Publications.

Suarez, Francis (1597). "Metaphysicarum Disputationum Tomi duo." tr. Copleston (1985), from I, 1, 24 in History of Philosophy, Vol. III. New York, New York: Doubleday.

Tompkins, James A., Ph.D. (1989). Winning Manufacturing: The How-To Book of Successful Manufacturing. New York, New York: McGraw-Hill, Inc.

Ulrich, W (1988). Critical Heuristics of Social Planning: A New Approach to Practical Philosophy. Berne, Switzerland: Verlay Paul Haupt.

Wallace, Robert H., Stockenberg, John E., & Charette, Robert N. (1987). A Unified Methodology for Developing Systems. New York, New York: Intertext Publications, Inc., McGraw-Hill, Inc.

Weinberg, G.H. (1975). An Introduction to General Systems Thinking. New York, New York: John Wiley & Sons.

Weitzen, H. Skip (1991). Hypergrowth: Applying the Success Formula of Today's Fastest Growing Companies. New York, New York: John Wiley & Sons.

Whitten, Neal (1990). Managing Software Development Projects: Formula for Success. New York, New York: John Wiley & Sons.

Wolf, Stephen M. (1990). "Editorial opinion," from U.S. Air Inflight Magazine, January, 1990, p. 14.

Yourdon, Edward (1986). Managing the Structured Techniques: Strategies for Software Development In the 1990's. Englewood Cliffs, New Jersey: Yourdon

Press.

——(1989). Modern Structured Analysis. Englewood Cliffs, New Jersey: Prentice-Hall.

——(1989b). Structured Walkthroughs. Englewood Cliffs, New Jersey: Yourdon Press.

Zwart, Martin (1990). Constraint-Driven Design Engineering. Amsterdam, The Netherlands: P.Q. Information Group, b.v.

These are exciting times for innovative executives as they face the new opportunities for success offered by the challenges of 21st Century competition. Systems Management Institute enjoys discovering the opportunities hidden in these challenges. Moreover, we receive great satisfaction from sharing the wealth of our experience, knowledge, and insights with our clients as they leverage their challenges to capture the emerging opportunities for success.

Systems Management Institute Credo

We enjoy working with leaders as they journey into the unchartered territory of 21St Century leadership. Although we accept the conventional wisdom that nothing under the sun is new, we also understand that the 21st Century business climate generates many challenges as opportunities that were scarcely imagined only a decade ago.

Systems Management Institute offers several carefully designed initiatives to bridge the old management paradigms with the new. We offer a powerful problem- solving environment for executives who feel a little uneasy about the continually emerging business environment, its trends, techniques, and assumptions. We advocate executive success, competency-based leadership, evolutionary guidance, and profitable growth. Our approach to executive assistance addresses four domains of the enterprise: (1) Cyber Security; (2) Systems Science; (3) Executive; (4) Information Technology, (5) Value Process Management. We work at the personal, team, and enterprise levels to assist clients with conquering many of their most pressing personal and professional challenges.

Our focus emphasizes the self-systems psychology of growth and the management of information technology during the Age of Cyber Security to attain competitive leverage. We know that today "sustainable competitive advantage" is another one of those business myths which have outlived their usefulness. We also know what to do about it. We excel at integrating theory with practice and balancing technical and social systems in the workplace. We are an innovative company who understands the practical realities of the competitive environment in the 21st Century.

Our Mission

We designed the Systems Management Institute with the complexities of today's world in mind, a world marked by the challenges of global systems trends which stretch the limits of earlier management approaches. We build executive success by introducing high performance strategic actions that link the domains of an enterprise to improve business value. As a leader in the design of Applied Intuitive Solutions™ Enterprise Architectures, SMI specializes in strategic innovation to empower executive action.

Serving both the public and private sectors, the SMI mission is fourfold: (1) Accelerate Business Value Realization; (2) assist executive with mastering the competencies required to lead successful enterprises well into the 21st Century; (3) increase the profitability of organizations through the application of Applied Intuitive Solutions™ empowered competency development Platforms and content, and (4) enhance executive knowledge of system thinking.

Our Clients

While the 20th Century's quest was for information and today's is about knowledge, tomorrow's quest will be for intelligence about business innovation and acceleration. Each quest demands an environment unique to itself. SMI is your bridge between the old and new paradigms and supports the business, organization, and technological interdisciplinary needs of clients including:

- Business owners and executives wishing to influence and improve the value of work teams through new Human Resource management strategies;
- Educators and corporate training managers wishing to develop a systems view essential for furthering research and instruction in the associated domains of Systems Inquiry;
- Business and technical managers wishing to shift to tomorrow's paradigms today;
- Clients wishing to reduce their business applications portfolios through the definition of Cyber Secure business rules;
- Consultants wishing to design unified business and security systems and broaden their methodology foundation, and
- Individuals interested in mastering the power of Design Inquiry.

Our Services

SMI recognizes that the need to make the paradigm shift is becoming more immediate as the trend toward embedded and more complex work teams increases. We have developed competency-based programs in coaching and leadership and have implemented Applied Intuitive Solutions™ Platforms to assist with the development of systems thinkers, executives, and leaders as practitioners of the emerging 21st Century business paradigms.

We offer a full range of coaching, consulting, and skills mastery solutions to facilitate the design of Insider Threat Prevention Cyber Security business architectures and competency-based programs in executive action. We offer rapid problem solving in 270 focus areas including Team Building, Workplace Relationships, Program and Project Management, Insider Threat Prevention Cyber Security,

Continuous Performance Management, Organization Change Management, Design Inquiry, Enterprise Design, and The Development of Virtual Commerce Trading Partner Agreements.

Organization Evaluations & Architecture Audits

These Evaluations and Audits enable clients to inexpensively avoid organization disasters by analyzing the suitability of project approaches and results. They inform clients of the hidden risks of current practices to enable clients to develop highly effective organizations appropriate to the environment, challenges, and situations they face. Our evaluations and audits provide rapid improvements in organization design, groupwork intensity, and team processes. They assess organization structure, job design, enterprise systems architectures, diversity, and staff selection and provide a powerful path for organization and leadership development.

"The organization of an organization reflects the organization of the people at the top." Mel Conway

Systems Management Institute
Orlando, Florida: (407) 864-7756
rnewkirk@smilc.info www.pblsol.com

Don't miss out!

Visit the website below and you can sign up to receive emails whenever Raymond Newkirk, Psy.D., Ph.D., Ph.D. publishes a new book. There' is no charge and no obligation.

https://books2read.com/r/B-A-ASCN-EAQLB

Connecting independent readers to independent writers.

About the Author

Dr. Raymond Leslie Newkirk is an internationally respected consulting specialist having earned advanced degrees and certifications in several disciplines including Ph.Ds. in the Philosophy of Science and Behavioral Science, Psy.D. in Clinical Psychology, Th.C., in Theology and the Ph.D. with Distinction in Human Science. Dr. Raymond

Leslie Newkirk originated the UlThule™ approach to human performance and the Applied Intuitive Solutions™ approach to problem solving. His professional background includes a distinguished career in multicultural research, human system design, and executive development. He has presented the Keynote Address to global audiences.

He is the Founder & CEO of the Systems Management Institute, a firm that applies human systems design to the building of high performance organizations. He was Founder and Chairman of Bay University, an innovative E-Learning Company. He has enjoyed a life-long interest in business and enterprise incubation. He founded his first company at the age of 16, a janitorial service with three employees, and has organized start-ups & joint ventures ever since.

Dr. Newkirk has served in diverse industries and executive capacities. He was a Senior Fellow of the Monterey Bay Management Group. He served as Chief Operating Officer of Mindmaker,Inc. San Jose, California, an early A/I and neural net pioneer that won Best of Comdex two years consecutively during the dot.com revolution in Silicon Valley. He also served as President and Chief Operating Officer of P.Q. Information Group, b.v. the Netherlands, an innovative company that pioneered Business Rules processing software development. He was the Founder of the International Association of Information Management (I-AIM).

He led projects for the Minister of Defense and Aviation and the Royal Saudi Naval Forces for the Kingdom of Saudi Arabia and for the Office of the President, Republic of the Philippines. Dr. Newkirk has led industry-changing engagements for Southwest Bell, Bank of America, and Dell Computers. He was a VIP Priority Guest of the CNN World Business Development Congress. He was invited as a visiting Ambassador in Business Development and Technology Transfer to the Soviet Union and as an expert guest to development conferences in Cairo, Egypt and Oxford, England. He conducted seminars for Technology Transfer, Rome, I.B.C. London and Amsterdam and S.I.B.C. Jeddah, Kingdom of Saudi Arabia.

Dr. Newkirk never stops writing. A prolific writer, he has published more than 3,600 articles, monographs, books, E-Learning courses, blogs, and guest columns for the San Francisco Examiner. His latest book, Navigating Sociopaths at Work, are now available worldwide. His book, Leading by Design, has become a widely sought collector's book that is available through the Systems Management Institute Press, Amazon, Barnes & Noble, or Booklocker Press. His most recent 4 book series, Insider Threat Prevention Cyber Security, presents a strategic model for unifying Continuous Performance Management with Insider Threat Prevention. It establishes the foundation for a new science that Dr. Newkirk refers to as Paleo-Leadership. He has authored works in English, Italian, Russian, Arabic, and Latin.

Dr. Newkirk advocates the intellectual, physical, and spiritual development of the person. He studied philosophy as a Benedictine Monk in Italy and studied theology with the Franciscan Friars in Washington D.C. He participated for many years with the Amateur Athletic Union (AAU) both as a competitor and supporter. Early in his athletic career, he attained international ranking in Olympic Weightlifting having won 12 championships and set 22 competitive records in the sport. He won Outstanding Weightlifter Award, Ohio State A.A.U. A few of his many records still stand today. Currently, he is in training to compete in the Masters World Championships and was the reigning Pacific Weightlifting Association Masters Champion where he is still in the business of chasing records. As an amateur explorer, Ray went diving in the Red Sea, mountain climbing in Alaska, worked as a deck hand on Dutch freighter, sailed in the Bahamas, and enjoyed deep-sea fishing in the Caribbean, among other global adventures.

Dr. Newkirk is an innovative social thinker. He is concerned about the problems facing the elderly in this technological and fast paced age. He has conducted workshops for senior citizens & executives on health, nutrition, and stress management. He established a health clinic and medical network for the elderly. He also contributed to the establishment of an orphanage in the Third World, funded fellowships for students in Eastern Europe to travel abroad and participate in seminars and professional training, and established a Southeast Asian International Fellowship.

Dr. Newkirk's Guiding Perspective is:

Life, Love, Leadership, Growth, & Honor "Live life fully. Love deeply with wisdom.

Lead others to great achievement.

Grow spiritually and intellectually.

Honor God in All You Do.

Don't miss out!

Visit the website below and you can sign up to receive emails whenever Dr. Raymond Leslie Newkirk publishes a new book. There's no charge and no obligation.

https://books2read.com/r/B-A-HJRKE-FBGYG

BOOKS 2 READ

Connecting independent readers to independent writers.

Did you love *21st Century Executive Life*? Then you should read *Adventures in Paleo Leadership*[1] by Raymond Newkirk, Psy.D., Ph.D., Ph.D.!

[2]

Leadership is a vital topic in every profession from. Business, Education, Government. and Defense to Religion, Science, Medicine, and Law Enforcement, and on and on and on. Leadership often makes the difference between success and failure. It is one of those topics that fuels the emotions of just about everyone from age ten to one hundred. Everyone seems to have an opinion about Leadership. These opinions frequently contradict one another as they generate confusion among followers. I wrote "Adventures in Paleo Leadership" to take us back, way way back, to that time when Leadership first began to emerge in recorded human affairs and follow its evolutionary unfolding to

1. https://books2read.com/u/mekZal

2. https://books2read.com/u/mekZal

better understand what Leadership is and how it became so confusing and complicated as it has become over the last several decades. From Mysticism to Psychology and all topics in between, Leadership has been part to the human landscape since human beings first started being together. ---- Raymond L. Newkirk

Also by Dr. Raymond Leslie Newkirk

21st Century Executive Life
21st Century Executive Life
21st Century Executive Life

Cosmic Truth God, Us and Them
Cosmic Truth: God, Us, and Them

Paleo-Leadership
Reconstructed Leadership

Standalone
A Person Passing By

www.ingramcontent.com/pod-product-compliance
Lightning Source LLC
LaVergne TN
LVHW090355210926
848480LV00002B/352